4 VIEWS ON PASTORING LGBTQ TEENAGERS
Effective Ministry to Gay, Bi, Trans, Queer, and Questioning Students Among Us

Mark Oestreicher, General Editor
Contributors:
Shelley Donaldson
Gemma Dunning
Nick Elio
Eric Woods

4 VIEWS ON PASTORING LGBTQ TEENAGERS

Copyright © 2018 by The Youth Cartel

Publisher: Mark Oestreicher
Managing Editor: Tamara Rice
Cover Design: Adam McLane
Layout: Marilee R. Pankratz
Creative Director: Tinky Winky

ISBN-13: 978-1-942145-36-3
ISBN-10: 1-942145-36-5

The Youth Cartel, LLC
www.theyouthcartel.com
Email: info@theyouthcartel.com
Born in San Diego
Printed in the U.S.A.

CONTENTS

INTRODUCTION

I'm going to be 100% transparent with you: *We want this book to change you.*

On one hand, we're not trying to "convert" you to a particular theology (unless that means that we want to "convert" you to a theology that truly loves teenagers in every conceivable category—gay, straight, bisexual, cisgender, transgender, gender fluid, queer, or simply wondering about one of these identity and gender issues). But it would be dishonest to imply we don't have an agenda in publishing this book as the first in our 4 Views series.

I mean, you bought this book from an organization called The Youth Cartel. You didn't actually think we'd be, uh… *tender*, did you?

We don't, however, have a liberal agenda (hidden or brazen). And we certainly don't have a conservative agenda. But we do have an agenda, and we want to be forthright about that.

We know for a fact that teenagers struggling with sexuality experience a way-higher-than-average amount of bullying. We know they consider suicide way more than average. And we know *Way Too Many* of them experience condemnation and judgment from the church.

We also know that for transgender teens, the percentages mentioned in the previous paragraph are even terrifyingly higher.

We know that for most gay and trans teens, the church is about the *least* safe place on earth. And we hope that in some way, this book will move the needle on that horrific reality.

I was particularly moved when reading the results of the largest study ever conducted on the faith of LGBTQ peoples (not just teenagers but all ages), reported in Andrew Marin's remarkable book, *Us Versus Us: The Untold Story of Religion and the LGBT Community* (NavPress,

2016). In short, one surprising finding of the study was that LGBTQ people score more than 10% higher than the general population when it comes to having a background in the Christian church (in America, that is). That fact itself is fascinating and worthy of reflection. The research team dug deep into the data, cross-referencing reams of data from other questions and digging into the responses from open-ended prompts.

They discovered that a large portion of *young teens* experiencing same-sex attraction (SSA) look for ways to rid themselves of the attraction they don't desire to have. Prior to their young teen years, survey respondents may have been aware of their SSA; but the questions (and often pain and fear) surrounding these issues become particularly urgent to young teens stepping into the developmentally normative work of identity formation.

Here's the news for youth workers (and churches in general): A statistically significant percentage of young teens experiencing SSA but *without* prior church experience turn to the church as a means of turning to God. Did you catch that? Young teens without prior church experience start attending church and/or youth programs specifically because of their SSA. They are looking, primarily, for answers and help (and often hoping that God will remove their SSA).

Sadly, the statistics also show that the vast majority of teens experiencing SSA *do not find help* in the church (all too often experiencing condemnation and rejection): The majority of LGBT adults report leaving the church (but not their faith) during their later teen years.

Teenagers are in our midst, looking for help; and we have been—for a very, very long time—failing them.

This is one of the reasons I am so firmly in agreement with Andy Stanley's insistence that the church should be the safest place to talk about anything, including SSA.

So we hope this book results in change. I know working on it has had a huge impact on me.

What This Book Isn't (And What It Is)

When The Youth Cartel decided to pursue a series of dialogue books around a four-views approach, we knew this topic had to be our first shot. This comes from the conviction, borne out of interactions with countless youth workers, that most in our tribe passionately want to be effective in ministry to teenagers but don't know how to proceed with LGBTQ young people.

But our observation was that there wasn't much to be gained by hosting another debate about what the Bible says (or doesn't say). There are *plenty* of other places to read about those debates—and we encourage you to read, listen, watch. Be informed about "both sides." (Really, it's essential that you compassionately understand how others who represent a biblical viewpoint divergent from yours think and interpret Scripture.) Instead, over and over again, we heard youth workers saying they needed more pragmatic help: *What do I do when a teenager comes out to me? How do I respond in a way that's helpful rather than creating additional problems?*

So this book is not a theological debate. We set out to find a handful of youth workers with experience in pastoring LGBTQ teens. We didn't want theory but practice. We didn't want propositions from someone who didn't actually know real-life LGBTQ teenagers; we wanted a collection of voices who have wrestled with these issues *because* they are involved with actual LGBTQ teenagers (and those teenagers' parents). We intentionally looked for a diversity of voices, which was a challenge that took roughly a year of conversations and dialogue.

We wanted this book to feel like you, the reader, are having a conversation with these four writers. Or at the least, we wanted you to be able to be a fly on the wall while the four of them had a meaningful conversation, one marked by compassion and respect.

This book is *not* intended to convert you to one of the four views represented. While each of the four writers believes strongly in their perspective (as they should), the tone is intentionally more "this is what I've learned" than "do this or you're an idiot."

A Surprise During Development (And What It Taught Us)

After working for so long to find four writers who were clearly different from one another in both experience and theological perspective, we were a little surprised to discover something as first drafts of chapters started to take shape. *Because* these writers are all relationally involved with real teenagers struggling with LGBTQ questions (and not merely standing on a soap box), we discovered that their suggestions were less differing than we'd assumed they would be. This revealed something critical that I'd like to now posit as an axiom here at the get go:

> *One cannot work out her approach to ministry with LGBTQ teenagers apart from relationships with real LGBTQ teenagers.*

I'd even go so far as to say that you and your church can't effectively work out your *theology* in this area apart from real relationships (even though theological or biblical frameworks are not the focus of this book). Most youth workers intuitively know this, though they may be under pressure to align themselves with a statement created by others. Youth workers, for the most part, are *practical theologians* not systematic theologians. Youth workers live in the real world with complicated, messy, passionate, beautiful teenagers and can't shake the divine compulsion to be missional, to meet real teenagers where they are, bringing a contextualized gospel to their world in hopes of having real teenagers connect with the real Jesus.

Ultimately, that's our hope for you: that you would be better equipped to help LGBTQ teenagers and those who are questioning or wondering connect with the real Jesus, rather than a polity or theological framework.

A Bit of Self-Exposure

As the general editor of this book, I think it's fair that I reveal some of my own journey (much of which I unpack in more detail in one of the two appendices). My own daughter, as a junior in high school, came out to me and my wife as bisexual. Months later, she told us that "bi" probably wasn't the full truth, that she was gay. About eighteen months later, Riley told us she was trans and wanted to take steps to transition to presenting as a male. And about six months after that, Riley settled on being gender neutral, using gender-neutral pronouns (they/their/them) and changing their name (Riley was Liesl). That was approximately five years ago.

As a result, my wife and I have walked this journey, not only as youth workers but as parents, from an extremely intimate and personal point of view. We've wrestled and cried and prayed and had a thousand conversations with our oldest child, who's now twenty-three years old (and many conversations with our younger son). We've spoken with our local youth ministry leaders, when Riley was still involved in the youth group. We've processed with national ministry leaders from a wide variety of perspectives. We've watched online videos and read many books, some of which were helpful and some of which were not. And I'll confirm right here that we have a wonderful and loving relationship with Riley and have learned so much from them. They were gracious and patient with us as we processed. (Shoot, even figuring out how to use plural pronouns took me a good two years!)

For many of these processing years, I said to those close to me that I didn't think "helping people figure out LGBTQ issues" was part of my calling and that I wanted to focus my ministry work on what God had clearly called me to. But as time has passed and I've had more and more and more conversations with youth workers who need help, I've realized that this *has become* part of my calling. I, Mark Oestreicher, want to help you, youth worker, in both understanding and practice. I want you to be better equipped to *not* add to the high percentage of questioning teenagers who leave the church because they've only experienced what they perceive as condemnation. (That "what they perceive" part is super important, and I'll unpack that a bit more in the appendix.)

So while I don't hope that this book converts you to a particular theology, I do hope—desperately—that this book will result in the teenagers you interact with experiencing a safe and loving mentor, a pastor (whatever your title or employment) who embraces them in the midst of their questions and provisional conclusions.

I invite you to read the pages that follow with an open mind (doing so is *not* a threat to your beliefs!), to read with compassion and a desire to learn. Allow Gemma, Nick, Shelley, and Eric to speak honestly with you. Know that they are not standing in judgment of you and they do not come to this armed for battle. They, along with me, invite you into dialogue, with the hope that God's Spirit would guide you.

– Mark Oestreicher
General Editor

VIEW 1: INTEGRITY AND IMAGO DEI

BY GEMMA DUNNING

I've been a sister, a physical one, longer than I've been a Christian. When my little sibling was born she was so small and precious, a tiny bundle of fragility that I swore as a big sister to protect and look after for all of my days. Little did I know that this would kick in much sooner than teenage bullies in the playground. She was a few weeks old when she got sick, really sick; and it looked like we might lose her, not just once but twice. To help us navigate this season we were given a sleep mat, a monitor that sounded an alarm whenever my sister stopped breathing, alerting us to a medical need and calling the whole family into action.

Living with this sense of impending doom had far bigger effects on the family. Even when the alarm was silent, we would all take turns watching the sleeping child, counting the breaths—always mindful, always checking in with each other: "Is she okay?" My big sister responsibility increased tenfold! Every scraped knee, every school report, there I was with her in it, right by her side.

Fast-forward to her late teens and, as a big sister, I maintained my sense of responsibility by repeatedly checking in with her—the annoying big sister always on her case, always asking awkward questions that more often than not, would result in me being told to "jog on." As we have grown up together, my love for her has only grown. That's what happens right? A unique bond bigger than anything; sisters journeying together through the best of times and the worst of times. I always thought of myself as a sister who would always have her back, no matter what, in it for the long hall, dedicated to her by nature of our very birth. Even if, as we grew, our beliefs shifted into different paths. We would always have each other, united in love. So, you can imagine my heartbreak when I happened to overhear her talking to her friend: "No, you just don't understand. I really can't tell her. You don't get it, she's, she's… religious. She'll hate me."

Crushed can't even begin to sum it up. Someone who knew me so well, who I thought knew I loved her 100% without any condition or agenda, actually thought that her very being would change the nature of our relationship. She believed, deep in her gut, that my faith would make her being gay too much for me. That it would be too big a risk to tell me something she'd been struggling alone with for fear that I would not just no longer love her but actually despise her. What could I have possibly done to make her feel that this would be my reaction?

Truth is there wasn't anything in particular. Nothing she could pinpoint apart from the usual "we all know what the church thinks." And yet in that context the most painful thing for me was that this was my sister, my flesh and blood. We weren't talking about someone I saw once a week; we were talking about someone who knew the very secrets of my heart, who was with me for every embarrassing childhood photo, and for whom this couldn't have been further from the truth. Surely she knew that I would always love her?

I couldn't wallow in the pain of this experience though; I had to see it for the call to action it was. For it quickly got me thinking: If she felt like this about me and she knows me, then what would those outside of my family think who didn't know me? What would my neighbors expect from me? And what message were the young people of our town hearing not just from me but from the wider church? It taught me that silence has its own voice—one that can cause damage and hold people hostage and is so often very different from the truth.

And as for my sister and I, well I bottled out the cringing conversation and texted her. It simply said:

> "I know you are gay. I love you. It doesn't change one thing about us. It will be okay."

MY JOURNEY

I've been a youth worker in the United Kingdom for the last nineteen years, working with a broad range of young people both within and outside of the church setting; but it wasn't until 2009 that I read Andrew Marin's story of building bridges from the church to the LGBTQ community, *Love Is an Orientation*, and suddenly woke up.[1] The words on its pages felt like a call for me to engage more actively in my own neighborhood of Bournemouth on the South Coast of England. It left me praying that perhaps God was calling others to stir up a movement of people in my neighborhood that could embody some of the outreach aspects of Marin's work. Bournemouth is recognized as being the fifth largest LGBTQ community in the UK—a physical piece of land just outside the town center that, despite being surrounded by churches, had no public contact with Christians outside of the Metropolitan Community Church (MCC) denomination. While the MCC was doing a grand job, I believed (and still do) that the kingdom of God was bigger and more diverse than any one denomination; and seeing a town full of churches who so publicly ignored a whole people group grated on me.

The grating increased; and in response to the discomfort God

---

1. Andrew Marin, *Love Is an Orientation: Elevating the Conversation with the Gay Community* (Grand Rapids, MI: IVP, 2009).

was laying on my heart I gave copies of Marin's book to lots of friends, all of whom had the potential to start a movement of change in the community. However, that didn't really go as well as I had hoped. Sure, people were moved by his words and by the vision that more could be done to love our neighbors; but the resounding cry came back: "When you start something, let us know and we'll join in."

The only problem was that I hadn't planned on starting anything. I'm actually averse to starting anything, to be honest. I have seen many a great "project" pop up and make a big splash only to lose steam, run out of money, or (far too often) lose its core leader. (Not to mention the reality that I have never really liked anything branded. The non-conformist in me likes the unique, bespoke individual; and to be a movement, there needs to at least be a hoodie and a brand for people to connect with, doesn't there?) So things went a bit quiet. I prayed that God would bring back a sense of peace and comfort, so I could carry on as I had been.

Then the little niggles became a big hurting mess right on my own doorstep, and it became hard to ignore God. I remember the day my son came home and told me what was happening at school. A student, one of his friends in an all-boys secondary school (for eleven- to eighteen-year-olds) was transitioning from male to female; and, to put it nicely, it wasn't the best of times for the student, the school, or the student's friends. And that student has their own story to tell. Perhaps they will at some point, but it's not for me to share anything else other than that watching this situation unfold around me was a catalyst for me. No longer could I sit back; I needed to learn more about LGBTQ issues to be able to guide my child as he loved and supported his friend. The youth worker within me knew I need some training; but back then—and sadly even today—there were very few resources to draw on.

The town has a great LGBTQ youth nonprofit, so I approached them and asked if I could volunteer. Naively, I thought they would jump at the chance of having a volunteer so experienced in youth work, but sadly this was not the case. I submitted my profile, which detailed my degree in theology and previous church-based experience. Being a non-religious organization, they didn't have a great working knowledge of the denominational structures we have; so, seeing that I was linked to a Baptist church, their only line of reference was to Westboro Baptist Church. As you can imagine, this proved for some interesting conversations—blunt ones, about agendas and whether I could separate my faith from my youth work practice. After much chatting, they could see it was unlikely I would be rocking up with a "God Hates Fags" banner; so thankfully they gave me a trial slot to see how we all felt about working together.

As they say, the rest is history. I went from volunteering once a week to twice a week, to being a staff member quite quickly. And I learned a lot from the fellow staff and the young people. But while I was learning a lot about LGBTQ issues and listening to lots of young people share their experiences and stories with me, there was still a black hole as far as youth work resources for me to draw from. So, as you do, I used some postgraduate work to seek answers to my own questions.

This drew me toward adapting an existing informal education theory in order to work with young people on a one-to-one basis as they wrestled with their faith and gender identity and/ or sexual orientation. It meant that most of the time I was a general LGBTQ youth worker working with a broad range of LGBTQ youth; but when the nonprofit was approached to support a young person of faith, I was the worker allocated to be their one-to-one support.

This experience means I have had too many teenagers to count sit before me with suicidal thoughts, self-harm scars, and internal heart wounds from theology that has told them their young selves are an abomination. I have met many beautiful, creative, gifted young people who are no longer able to serve in any capacity in their churches because they had the integrity to share with their church leader about their same-sex feelings. And sadly, I have met too many young people who—despite no actual sexual experience with anyone—have been refused sacraments such as communion and baptism.

As an evangelical, I am passionate about seeing young people encounter the fullness of life offered by Jesus. My heart's desire though is not just merely to see young people survive, but to equip and enable them to thrive. However, my experience tells me that for many LGBTQ young people, the church is not a source of flourishing. I am eternally grateful for that brilliant nonprofit and their committed bunch of youth workers—many of whom are volunteers giving back to either repay support they themselves had or to be the change in the lives of others after lacking support in their own journeys. They have modeled time and time again what it is to put young people's welfare at the heart of the matter, and they are literal lifesavers.

This then led to many beautiful experiences. From leading "Carols and Cocktails" in a local bar to repeated involvement with the local pride parade to being part of some truly moving vigils. My LGBTQ neighbors became my friends—friends who knew I was a Christian and, as such, would ask me to do Christian things like pray, respond in pastoral situations, share wisdom and advice, and lead community events.

As our relationships shifted from neighbors to friends, it also had some unforeseen side effects and gifted me with a community that stood by me and my family when we needed support. In fact, my first term's worth of fees at Bristol Baptist College, as I studied for training as a Baptist minister, were paid for by Bournemouth's Bourne Free Committee—that's the committee who organize the local gay pride parade and events around it. I believe this is a first and not a headline many would expect to hear. And it is from this experience that I have just moved to London to be a minister within the Baptist Union of Great Britain, a church and denomination with a core value of inclusion that is expressed in a variety of ways.

On the side, over the last few years, I have also been a pastoral facilitator for Diverse Church, a UK-based online support network of over a thousand LGBTQ Christians (and their parents), many of whom are under thirty years old. And I have supported a number of LGBTQ Christian organizations—such as Christians at Pride and Affirm, a UK network of Baptist Christians working together for LGBTQ inclusion.

But, sadly, not many friends from the church have come along with me on this adventure. This mission has led to being cut off, removed, and—at times—ridiculed among my would-be Christian peers. I have been uninvited from speaking at events, uninvited from children's christenings, and had more than the average struggle to find a place in ministerial training—proving that the wider expression of church still has some really big issues around this topic to wrestle with in the days ahead.

WHAT DRIVES MY VIEW

Along the way, in my journey, I have picked up a few tidbits, learned some hard lessons, and had to ask big internal questions about how I personally respond to young people who identify as LGBTQ and all the letters we often leave out. To be clear, I'm not going to exposite Scripture and pull out the usual passages, as there has already been much written on this. Nor can I provide all the answers to all the questions you may have; this is just one chapter. I can, on the other hand, offer some reflections that have been, for me, key areas of learning, key concepts that have pushed my ministry in the direction it's gone. These are the ideas that integrity ought to matter to Christians as much as we say it does and that if we say we are all made in the image of God—the *Imago Dei*—then we must affirm that LGBTQ individuals are also made in the image of God.

However, it's important for you to note that since I'm far from perfect, my reflections on living out these concepts are far from perfect. Each and every day I am still on a journey, learning something new and heading in a new direction from and with the beautiful humans God has grafted into my life. Missionary Vincent Donovan quotes wise words from a young collegiate in his book, *Christianity Rediscovered*:

> "In working with young people, do not try to call them back to where they were, and do not try to call them to where you are, as beautiful as that place may seem to you. You must have the courage to go with them to a place that neither you nor they have ever been before."[2]

Integrity and Imago Dei: Full Disclosure

In our evangelical circles, we talk a lot about the importance of having integrity and being open to the concept of being fully known to those who disciple us. It's paramount to any individual's growth and development, particularly in the teenage years when young people are learning, making mistakes, and testing boundaries. And yet, often when our young people disclose who they are in all their LGBTQ-ness, despite modeling true integrity in that moment, we, the church, fail to thank them for that integrity and honesty. Often, at best, we reduce our conversations to whispers in the shadows, monitoring their friendships and relationships, filtering the leadership opportunities we give them, and praying they don't sign up for summer camp so we don't have to have those awkward "which room" conversations. At worst, we the people of God can so often make it hard for the young person to remain in the life of the church. So much so that they leave, often without a sense of faith to hold on to and losing many of their church-based friends en route.

As youth workers, all too often our response can be to jump far too quickly to trying to fix the issue; and that, more often than not, means we fail to acknowledge what guts and courage it takes a young person to speak up. Disclosing a deeply personal truth to someone who sits in a place of power and position over them takes a lot of courage. Now, I know some of you are thinking, "Hold on. I don't have any

---

2. Vincent J. Donovan, *Christianity Rediscovered: An Epistle from the Masai* (London: SCM Press, 1982) p. vii.

power." And perhaps that's how you see yourself, but to a young person attending a group where you are a worker, paid or not, you do have power by default. And more than this, you are often a worker who is also a peer to their parents, older siblings, life-long family friends, teachers, community leaders, etc. By confiding in you, there is much at risk for that young person; and, as such, we need to not just assume they know we are thankful to them for trusting us with a part of themselves. Instead we need to actively say something to them about it. In matters of LGBTQ-ness, the silence and the words we fail to speak can have such devastating unintended effects.

I firmly believe that the church should be the safest place for a young person to talk about anything— including (but not exclusively) LGBTQ topics. If a young person has come

> "Disclosing a deeply personal truth to someone who sits in a place of power and position over them takes a lot of courage."

to you, it is because they feel safe enough to do so. So before you respond to any young person about your own theological stance, the stance of the church, or even suggest praying together in response, we need to—as youth workers—thank, if not physically applaud, young people for modeling to us the very thing we talk so much about: *integrity.* They need to hear that the sleepless nights, the stressed-out days, and the weeks rehearsing every possible outcome of this action were not in vain. As such, take a disclosure of this nature as a youth work win. Applaud and champion young people who are able to have these difficult conversations with you and credit them by modeling some integrity back.

Integrity and Imago Dei: Our Response

"What? Model it back? What does that look like in this context?" I can almost hear you asking. Well, here is the biggest thing I have learned over the last decade in youth ministry...

> *It is absolutely fine to acknowledge to a young person that you don't know everything about everything.*

They might use terms you don't understand; it's okay to ask them what they mean by those terms. They may say things you don't understand; it is absolutely fine to ask, "Could you tell me more about that or describe how this makes you feel?" You are not expected to know everything about everything—and that includes how every single member of your church or community might respond to this discussion.

What is important though is that you model back integrity; if you don't know the answer to a question they have then *say so*. But this doesn't mean that we shouldn't think about how we phrase our responses. When a young person comes out to you, often they want to know what impact this will have on being part of your group or their serving in your organization. It is very different to respond with "Oh, right, erm, yeah, erm, I'm not sure how that's going to work out here..." than with...

> *Thank you so much for sharing this with me. I appreciate that it takes a lot of courage to share something of yourself, and I am thrilled and honored you chose to share this with me. Know that God already is present to this information; he knows you and he loves you, and here we know you and we love you, and this information doesn't change that. I'm not sure what everyone else thinks or what discussions around this have already happened, so I don't have all the answers to all the specifics right now. But if you want, we can find out together.*

This also means though that we need to have the integrity to not set up young people to fail. If we know our churches are not safe places to be known, then we need to support young people in making connections with people and organizations outside of our churches.

This might terrify you. I know a lot of my youth work buddies were really shocked when I started spending time with local non-Christian support agencies, but it is important that we keep the young person's well-being at the core of what we do. I have heard so many young people talk about being the "only one" and feeling isolated, lonely, and disconnected. But as youth workers we have the power to connect young people to others who have more knowledge than we do, who have different areas of experience, and who have wider networks of support. Neither our holiness nor the young person's holiness is altered by seeking support outside of the church. Moreover, stepping outside the walls of the church offers an opportunity for us to learn alongside the young person, meeting new people together and sharing first experiences together.

If we know our church has already had discussions around these issues and the young person is going to have a tough time staying connected to our community, then we need to consider how we are going to support that young person spiritually in the days ahead. Occasionally we are in positions to be able to speak to those people who make the decisions, and we have voices that can broker new ground for young people who ordinarily wouldn't get their voices heard. Sometimes though, the best thing we can do for young people is to support them in finding an affirming faith community to plug into with our blessing.

I've had to do this a few times, and it is heartbreaking to have to admit that your faith community is not a space where someone will thrive. Not everyone is called to pioneer through the tough experimental phase of being the only person who's different; and as you read this, I'm sure you'll be thinking of different communities you have been a part of and will call to mind examples where transitioning to a new, affirming church would be the best option.

But what this doesn't have to mean is closing a door on the young person. We live in a transient world, where people can change churches and

> "Neither our holiness nor the young person's holiness is altered by seeking support outside of the church."

not disappear off the face of the planet. This can be made easier by making friends with ministers and youth workers of churches that are explicitly affirming. Not only being able to call on their advice when you need to but—more than that—offering them friendship, loving them well, praying with and for them, and being church with them is vital. My experience has taught me immensely about how much it means to have people in my life who might not agree with me on every theological point there is but who, despite our differences, still love me, stand with me, and are church to me in the ordinary, everyday bits of life.

Fearfully and Wonderfully Made

Many young people inside the church grow up hearing time and time again how they are made in the image of God. It is all around them from the moment they are born—the cute posters in the Sunday school room to bookmarks their mothers give them.

If you grow up in the church, you are saturated in the knowledge that you are fearfully and wonderfully made. Spoken over you is the truth that God knows you inside out and back to front. However, there are times when, on the journey, many LGBTQ youth feel this shifts for them. The church—that is, the people in the church—stop celebrating that the LGBTQ youth is made in God's image and start instead asking questions of them as if God is not aware of their orientation or full identity. It seems that, as leaders, we can struggle to affirm that some people are "queerfully" and wonderfully made. Perhaps even reading that phrase is jarring for you. It is too much of a concept for you to grasp.

However, I am convinced that if we hold on to a God who knows each and every hair on our heads, then he also knows who we find attractive; and all of that is wrapped up in a package that still reflects the image of God. Now read me right: I am talking about people as human beings; I am not talking about when we engage in *acts* that might be seen as sinful. Instead, I am referring to our very rawest, purest nature of simply *being*.

Yet sadly, it can seem as if we separate out categories in church far too often: those who are made in the image of God and those who are not. Historically this has been linked to all manner of sin, yet mostly it is allocated as a label when any manner of sexual sin has occurred. Perhaps you feel this is too harsh a criticism of the church, but many of the LGBTQ young people I have worked with have found themselves on the receiving end of this categorizing. Sometimes this has been explicitly declared—physical words spoken over them by pastors, youth workers, and parents, heard from pulpits and discussed at conferences. Other times it can present as more subtle and implicit—the pity look; being treated as less-than-equal compared to peers; and often in the silencing of views, opinions, and prayers as if these young people have nothing of value, of God, to contribute.

Of course, I do understand the pastoral tensions this presents when you are attempting to call all of the church to a higher level of holiness, but I can't help but reflect that when we do this, either deliberately or unintendedly, we reduce God. When we find ourselves doing this, we limit the Creator of the Universe, who is omnipresent and omnipotent. A young person doesn't need to tell God and have a formal discussion with him regarding their sexuality or gender identity, for this has already been an ongoing known conversation—often for many years before we are drawn into the conversation.

It is often at this point in the journey where "love the sinner, hate the sin" is brought into the conversation—something I'll unpack more when we talk practicalities. How-

"Yet sadly, it can seem as if we separate out categories in church far too often: those who are made in the image of God and those who are not."

ever, did you know that many believe this statement to be a rephrasing by Ghandi, an adaptation of a quote originally spoken by St. Augustine, which said "with love for mankind and hatred for sins"?[3] And yet I still hear it used by Christians on a weekly if not daily basis as if it is chapter and verse from the Bible.

So how can we reconcile that God has already known someone's gender identity or sexual orientation since they were created, before they even knew it themselves? Moreover, with this in mind and not in

---

3. Jonathan Merritt. "One Problem with Kim Burrell's Hate the Sin, Love the Sinner Argument," January 4, 2017: https://www.usatoday.com/story/news/2017/01/04/kim-burrell-hate-the-sin-love-the-sinner/96158416/.

spite of it, God has knitted them together as fearfully and wonderfully made. So, what does it look like to affirm who LGBTQ young people are in light of this? How can we shape a youth ministry to treat young LGBTQ people with this sense of inherently divine dignity?

I sometimes have more questions than answers to these questions. But I do know that far too often when we talk about "loving the sinner and hating the sin" we fail big time to actually love *the human* at the heart of the matter, never mind to acknowledge the divine in them, their *Imago Dei*.

GETTING PRACTICAL

Shifting towards a more practical approach, I find the words of a youth worker buddy of mine, Ricky, a useful encouragement: "Nothing that happens changes who God is or how he responds to me. Everything that happens can change who I am and how I respond to God." So, for me, I seek to give space for all those young people I journey with to reflect the image of God to me, affirming that they are made in his image and have the spark of the divine at their very core. This doesn't change, ever. Even when they might be engaging in behavior that I don't like or don't think is the best for them, this still remains at the core of our relationship.

This means, as a youth worker, I need be mindful to actively curate space for the divine to speak through them—not just in our one-to-ones but corporately too, for us a community to hear what they feel God has to say and to ensure that they are given the same opportunities to spiritually plug into God that every other teen is being given.

Many of the LGBTQ teens I have had the privilege to work alongside have shown me deep, new insight into the Scriptures; brought new aspects to justice; and demonstrated brave and courageous actions in the name of solidarity and love. The church is richer for hearing, seeing, and being a part of this type of faith; and the LGBTQ aspect of the body is one the rest of the body would do well to take more note of instead of easily dismissing it as unneeded or, at worst, illegitimate.

Demonstrating Love

This year as a church we have been camped out in the Sermon on the Mount: those few chapters of Matthew where Jesus pulls the crowd together to challenge them on how to live life in the kingdom, the series of "you have heard it said, but I tell you…" verses reminding us that the words we read in the Bible or hear in sermons are often meaningless unless they generate action. It has been a challenge—it has been a life-long challenge for some of us—to get our words to match our actions and to see bigger, broader narratives when those around us want defined answers on specifics. (And besides, if we are honest, we're living in an entirely different context now than when the Word was formed, so the answers to the specifics in question often aren't found within the Scriptures.)

See, we talk about loving one another as Christ has loved us, but what does it look like to model it to those young people who identify as LGBTQ? What really happens when we use phrases like "love the sinner and hate the sin"? And how can we practice what we preach, that all are known and loved by God? The world is looking on, watching and waiting to see how we treat each other in our differences and looking for good, healthy models of love. This often generates more questions though than answers.

> "See, we talk about loving one another as Christ has loved us, but what does it look like to model it to those young people who identify as LGBTQ?"

Just last week I was with a small group of young women in central London when one asked me, "How can you tell if someone is a Christian?"

Now, the context of this is important: It was London Pride, a day when LGBTQ people are in high numbers in our city. And on this day a group of around ten men in their mid- to late-fifties had chosen to bring placards with clobber verses into the city. They had bullhorns and PA systems with them; and they were shouting rather loudly and somewhat intimidatingly not just to the small group I was with but everyone who happened to be passing by.

This didn't go down too well with the general public walking past; and many of them sought to argue back—which, of course, only insured a louder response, generating more reaction, which spiralled into a vicious circle. At certain points it felt as if violence might ensue and, as such, the police joined us on the street for the afternoon to keep everyone safe.

The whole experience left the three young women I was with somewhat bewildered, particularly as I, their minister, deployed my best distraction tactics: giving away sweets to those passing by and trying to encourage them to not argue with the protesters but to go and have a thoroughly lovely day. (How very English, eh?) But it brought up some valid reflections from the young people: *How do we tell who has received redemption from the Lord? What does it look like to love others well?* and *Where was God in all of that?*

Mindful that we are not to judge, I asked the young women to retell things as they saw it. They believed the protesters to be angry people, recognizing that some of what was said was personally nasty and revealed sweeping judgements about people they did not know, including them. But they could also recognize that when you love someone and they do something that you feel is harmful to themselves then this can (and does) make you angry. They had also seen the impact the group had on people: some crying, some getting angry, some laughing at them and mocking them. This left these women more confused than when we started but gave them some insight into the tension the church finds itself in. Even if we think our motives for doing something are right it doesn't make it right to those on the receiving end.

There is a difference between what we *intend* to do and what consequences our actions have. These fellas were not giving the impression of love, even if it was love that was their driving motive. (By the way, they weren't up for a conversation around this; nor did they take the Skittles I offered them.) And as I said before, all the while the world was watching on.

What this did do was to give some space to talk about the ministry of Jesus: how radical it was that his followers *included* those that the religious right sought to *exclude*; how revolutionary the stories of Jesus physically touching and being touched by women would have been at the time; and how the Gospels show us how Jesus responded to those who found themselves on the margins and offer insight into how we could model ourselves on him. Sure, Jesus probably would have taken the Skittles and made a bit extra, and quite possibly there would have been a bit more physical contact with strangers. (Though safeguarding is important for most of us humans in such situations.) But the women quite quickly identified that much of Jesus' interactions mirrored the qualities described in the fruits of the spirit.

> "There is a difference between what we *intend* to do and what consequences our actions have."

In his book, *The Great Spiritual Migration*, Brian McLaren says:

> "Of the many radical things said and done by Jesus, his unflinching emphasis on love was the most radical of all. Love was the greatest commandment, he said (Matthew 22:37-40). It was his new commandment, his prime directive—love for God, for self, for neighbor, for stranger... and even for enemy, as he himself modeled. The new commandment of love meant neither beliefs nor words, neither taboos, systems, structures nor the labels that enshrined them mattered most. Love decentered [and] relativized everything else; love took priority over everything else."[4]

It is by our love for one another that we will be known (John 13:35), but the love that Jesus calls for looks very different from a love that

---

4. Brian D. McLaren, *The Great Spiritual Migration: How the World's Largest Religion Is Seeking a Better Way to Be Christian* (New York: Convergent, 2016), 41-42.

takes us down the charity road. For often in our natural desire to be nice, pleasant, and a peacekeeper our "charity" morphs into "fixing something for someone quickly" in order to move forward happily with little to no fuss or disruption—as if it never happened at all. (Or perhaps that's just my Britishness coming out!) Rather, as Maya Angelou said, "Love recognizes no barriers. It jumps hurdles, leaps fences, penetrates walls to arrive at its destination full of hope."[5] This kind of love has some edge to it—something assertive, aggressive about it even—but this can leave us a bit confused by what a loving presence looks like in our weekly youth groups.

So, with this in mind, I asked some young LGBTQ people to share their real-life experiences of receiving life-changing love from within the churches; and here is what they said:

> "Listening well and asking me genuine questions about my sexuality, then still asking me if I would be up for playing drums in the worship band."

> "Reminding me of events and making it clear that I am missed when I am not around."

> "My church has a thing that is read out before communion sometimes about how welcome everyone is. It includes a bit, which is something along the lines of 'we welcome everyone whether they love the same sex, the opposite sex, both sexes or none.' It's amazing to see that church could be even more inclusive than even some LGBTQ support groups."

> "The youth workers stopped saying 'guys' all the time to get the attention of the group and started using more gender-neutral terms like 'friends' and 'do you have anyone special in your life?' rather than assuming everyone has someone of the opposite gender in their life or that they fancy."

---

5. "13 of Maya Angelou's Best Quotes," *USA Today* (online), May 28, 2014: https://www.usatoday.com/story/news/nation-now/2014/05/28/maya-angelou-quotes/9663257/.

"Reading books on LGBTQ faith with me to learn together."

"Showing an interest into other areas of my life, asking about school, friends, sports—normal everyday things—and not always focusing on me being gay."

"My youth worker offered to come with me when I mentioned I wanted my hair cut at the barbers for the first time but was scared to go alone."

If you were to boil down the takeaways here, the lessons for all of us would be:

1. **Be explicit in your welcoming of LGBTQ teens.** Church, God, and faith is for all.

2. **Use inclusive language that doesn't make assumptions about sexual orientation.** What we say can alienate or it can invite.

3. **Show an interest in all aspects of the young person's life, not just their LGBTQ status and struggles.** Adolescence is still adolescence. Don't ignore ordinary feelings, wins, and struggles.

4. **Connect youth to affirming books, theological resources, and autobiographies.** It's important that they know many Christians affirm who they are, many have been where they are, and they are not alone.

5. **Be physically present for your LGBTQ teens as a support and champion.** Look for ways to come alongside them, even stepping into roles that other adults in their life may have abandoned.

Offering Solidarity Rather than Charity

The quotes I've shared from LGBTQ young people help to articulate something which has become very important to my own sense of calling as a minister, and I've touched on it here once already. Often as a body of people, the church is keen to engage in acts of charity.

We get moved by heart-wrenching stories, and our humanity calls us to act in response. The trouble is, this acting is often within a measured response: We give what we can afford; we go to one event; we are moved to demonstrate pity to those in front of us who are experiencing hardship.

Charity is a short-term action that enables the person with the power to do something to feel temporarily better. But I do believe God is calling us to more, that we are called to be a people who minister out of solidarity rather than charity. Solidarity offers a more horizontal approach. *Solidarity* recognizes that regardless of power structures other may seek to impose, two individuals both have something to learn from one another, both have value, both deserve dignity and opportunity; and together, united in our approach, we can achieve far more than we could ever imagine alone. I believe that this approach is both long overdue and well needed.

For many of our LGBTQ teenagers, the truth is that life remains extremely difficult, even in these unprecedented days when equality and acceptance has never been this high, when many have the option of marriage and family, and many workplaces have policies in place to protect LGBTQ employees. I'm sure many of you will be aware of the stats in your region for LGBTQ bullying, homelessness, and even suicide.

In the UK, the most recent report by the research and advocacy group Stonewall reflects the experiences of LGBT young people in Britain's schools and identifies some alarming statistics that include:

- Nearly half of lesbian, gay, bisexual, and transgender pupils (45%) including sixty-four percent of transgender pupils—are bullied at school for being part of the LGBTQ community.
- More than four in five trans young people (84%) have self-harmed. For lesbian, gay, and bisexual young people who aren't transgender, three in five (61%) have self-harmed.
- Nearly one in ten transgender pupils (9%) are subjected to

death threats at school.

- More than half of LGBTQ pupils (53%) say that there isn't an adult at school they can talk to about their sexual orientation or gender identity.

- Just two in five LGBTQ young people (40%) have an adult at home they can talk to about issues around their gender identity and/or sexual orientation.

- More than two in five trans young people (45%) have attempted to take their own lives. For lesbian, gay, and bisexual young people who aren't transgender, one in five (22%) have attempted to take their own lives.[6]

LGBTQ youth now, more than ever, need youth workers committed to ensuring they don't just survive but have the opportunity to thrive (John 10:10). In fact, I believe

"LGBTQ youth now, more than ever, need youth workers committed to ensuring they don't just survive but have the opportunity to thrive..."

God is calling a movement of people to stand in solidarity with LGBTQ teens and their families. A movement of people who are committed to faithfully loving them as Christ has loved us, regardless of whether the young person acts on their orientation or not. Seeking to maintain and even curating opportunities for them to continue to explore all aspects of discipleship, including leading and teaching, if they feel called. Offering learning opportunities for students and parents in how to support LGBTQ youth and not shying away from or fudging the questions young people have about issues of sexuality and gender identity. We need a movement of people who call the larger church to celebrate *all* the young people in their care and who stand with young people and families who need support in practical presence, not abandoning them when things become difficult or

---

6. Josh Bradlow, Fay Bartram, April Guasp and Dr. Vasanti Jadva. "School Report: The Experiences of Lesbian, Gay, Bi, and Trans Young People in Britain's Schools in 2017," Stonewall and the Centre for Family Research, University of Cambridge, 2017: https://www.stonewall.org.uk/sites/default/files/the_school_report_2017.pdf.

matters are made public.

FINAL THOUGHTS

Ministering to any young person has its quirks, but ministering to LGBTQ youth, in particular, will be a journey full of its own challenges. Chances are it won't win you accolades; and it is guaranteed to upset others, just as Jesus' ministry did. It means people will misunderstand your intentions, make assumptions about you, and they might even question whether you even have a theological framework at all. It is likely to mean that God may call you into spaces and situations that make you feel uncomfortable, out of your depth, and beyond your own knowledge. For sure, it will leave you with way more questions than answers, but the journey will not be dull. For it will bring more color and dimension to your ministry in the most unimaginable ways as you start to see things through different perspectives and encounter the difference personally.

Remember that for one young person you may just be a miracle, a lifeboat that reminds them of the true Lighthouse Keeper: someone who manifests incarnate characteristics when all around them speak another story, someone who brokers hope for the days ahead.

RESPONSE

BY ERIC WOODS

In her very personal story of discovering her own sibling's struggle with faith, family, and her own sexuality, Gemma reveals a reality that should undoubtedly be becoming clear to the reader: More and more, our views on the topic of ministry to people in the LGBTQ community are informed by personal relationships. In fact, a significant portion of the American public now has a close friend or relative who is openly gay, transgender, or queer.

A person's story and experience is a very personal matter—one that cannot be debated, minimized, or ignored. And Gemma's is an experience I do not share. I can't imagine the pain her family endured during those early days of medical uncertainty when her sister was born, and I cannot imagine the pain of rejection her sister felt (or feared) surrounding her sexuality. And yet, we must be careful to not allow our experience to become our final authority on matters of faith and practice.

Undoubtedly for many—perhaps for Gemma, as well—it was the realization of a close personal friend or family member's struggle with sexuality that shifted their views on the matter from one of *acceptance* to one of *affirmation*.

In fact, the question which Gemma's experience raised is one I agree everyone in ministry should answer: *What message are the young people of our town hearing not just from me but from the wider church?* And it's here where our views diverge. For even though we agree that church should be a safe place—and although I advocate an approach that seeks to *affirm* young people wherever possible—we cannot and should not affirm attitudes and behaviors inconsistent with our understanding of Scripture.

Further, while we agree that *all* are made in the image of God

(LGBTQ and otherwise), we mustn't forget that, sadly, we live in a fallen world. Therefore, I don't believe any of us accurately reflects that image.

If we agree that God doesn't make mistakes—and I think we do—and if one starts from a position that people are "made" gay or trans or queer, then one must accept that God intentionally made them gay or trans or queer… a position which necessitates affirmation.

However, if one is willing to acknowledge that, maybe, God made that person and somehow, *apart* from his plan and purpose (I don't think we yet know how or why), they identify as gay or trans or queer, then one could also accept that maybe God could also *remake* that person. *Remaking* is what he promises all of us so that ultimately, over time, we will each more accurately reflect his image (2 Corinthians 3:18).

When I was in middle school, my parents' marriage fell apart, resulting in their divorce. It was a terribly difficult time for my family, and for a long time it caused me to question God's decision to use marriage as a picture of Christ's love for the church (Ephesians 5:25). It seemed that, since so many marriages fail, this was a poor choice of metaphor.

But we don't reject the image of Christ's love in marriage because of the prevalence of broken marriages. Nor do we affirm that divorce (God hates divorce, per Malachi 2:16) somehow reflects Christ's love for the church. In the same way, we should not feel that because a person is created in God's image, we must affirm that *everything* about that person—in this case, their sexuality—reflects it.

My ultimate goal in ministry is to see young people live lives of consistent holiness and increasing Christlikeness. Because of this, I believe we do need to make the church a place where they feel that they belong and where they come for primary support as they walk an often lonely road. We need to invite and encourage them to stay engaged with the church, even though the church may not "affirm" their sexual identity.

Absolutely, LGBTQ youth must be given the same opportunities to spiritually plug into God as every other teen is being given. They must be given the same opportunities to worship, to study, to learn, to grow, to confess, to seek God, to doubt, to ask questions, and to be challenged. And we owe it to them to faithfully walk with them on their journey towards greater Christlikeness.

VIEW 2: UNITY OVER UNIFORMITY

BY NICK ELIO

One Sunday, I was hanging out with some of our students and leaders when another staff person came to me and said there was a family that wanted to speak with me about our student ministry at Denver Community Church (DCC). I excused myself from my conversation and saw a father and daughter standing up the aisle from me. As I walked towards them, my brain started doing what *all* our brains do in the seconds leading up to meeting new people. I was taking in all the visual information I could.

The dad was average age for having a teenager, dressed normally for a Sunday at DCC, nothing too particular about him.

His daughter—probably late middle school, seventh or eighth grade—was dressed in fairly "alternative" clothing. Dark eye makeup with a choker necklace and short, pixie-cut, dyed-black hair. Like you may be doing now, I was making some assumptions about her based on her fashion sense.

I introduced myself, "Hi! I'm Nick, the student ministries pastor here at DCC. It is nice to meet you both." That's when they told me their names were Doug and Daisy,[1] and I asked Daisy what grade she was in.

She said, "Seventh."

I asked them how long they had been coming to our church, and they told me that it was their very first Sunday. Then I asked them what brought them to DCC, and the conversation slowed down a bit. Doug turned to his daughter, seemingly to ask her permission, which she granted by giving him an affirmative head nod. I had an immediate sense of what was coming next as DCC had just announced our decision to move to full inclusion of the LGBTQ community the week prior. (We'll get to that later...)

Doug turned back to me and said, "Well, Daisy is gay."

I turned to Daisy and said, "I'm really happy that you are here." Then asked, "How long have you known?"

"Since I was seven," she replied.

I then asked Doug how long *he* had known. "Since last week," he said with a smile and a laugh.

At that, we all chuckled a bit, acknowledging that as a family, they were living in a *whole* new reality as of very recently. I then asked a question I felt confident I knew the answer to: "What brought you to DCC?"

Doug said, "We heard about your decision for full inclusion of the LGBTQ community; and when Daisy came out to her mother and me last week, we knew we couldn't go back to our church."

When I heard that, I knew the pain and hurt they must have been carrying. I turned to Daisy and said, "I'm so sorry..." Her eyes began

---

1. **Editor's Note:** All names of LGBTQ teens and their family members in View 2 have been changed by the writer to protect the privacy of the minors involved.

to fill with tears, which of course meant *my* eyes filled with tears. I continued, "I'm sorry if anyone has ever made you feel like you aren't welcome in church, and I'm so glad you are here."

Changing Perspectives

In Denver, the Rescue Mission sits on the corner of a three-way intersection as Broadway cuts through the cross streets of Park Avenue and Lawrence at a forty-five-degree angle. Which means there is an island, a triangle-shaped median where those in the homeless community gather, waiting to line up for food and a bed. In college I would head downtown every Sunday night with a group of friends to spend time with those who were experiencing homelessness in our city. We would load up one hundred peanut butter and jelly sandwiches or as many hotdogs as we could fit in our backpacks, along with a five-gallon jug of powdered lemonade, to simply walk around, hand out food, and have conversations.

One of those conversations was with a man named Tim. Tim was in his fifties and living on the street. Months earlier Tim had been the general manager of a local business making six figures a year. He had a house in the suburbs with a wife and kids, yet there he sat. Tim had fallen on some tough times; and due to a remarkable series of unfortunate events, with very little extended family or savings to fall back on, he had lost his job, his house, and then his wife. As I learned more about how Tim ended up waiting in line for a bed at the Rescue Mission, many of my stereotypes and presuppositions about how and why people ended up homeless were challenged.

Maybe you've had a similar experience with those in the homeless community, or those with addiction, or maybe you were on a mission trip to Mexico or South America where something you previously used to think and talk about as if it were just an *issue* suddenly got real.

Real people.

Real stories.

Real families.

Maybe you came to realize during an "urban immersion" experience or on a trip to a country that is supposedly so much more "poor" than the US, that we are not actually talking about homelessness or immigration or poverty as *issues*. We discover through relationship, through conversation, and through experience that we are actually talking about *people*; and from that moment on we know everything about that topic will never be the same. Before my Sunday nights in front of the Rescue Mission, I held some fairly negative assumptions about the homeless community. But then I met people like Tim and learned. This wasn't a bad guy. He wasn't a drunk, and he most certainly wasn't choosing to be homeless. He was not a repeat offender, nor was he some bum who was "too lazy to get a job." He was a person, just like you and me; and his situation was not that far outside the realm of possibilities for any one of us.

When it comes to LGBTQ youth, so easily this conversation can feel like an "issue" in the church today. Something that needs to be figured out or solved. But we need to remember that when we are having the "LGBTQ conversation," we are talking about people, students, and families. We are talking about sons and daughters, moms and dads, brothers and sisters. Teenagers in our ministries and communities, who for a long time may not have felt heard. Friends who have lived in fear or who have felt they needed to hide who they really are because they were not sure how others would respond.

There are plenty of books debating the merits of the many theological positions of this conversation; but here, for this project, we need to remember this is about people. It is so easy in our world today to be dualistic—Democrats vs. Republicans, Conservatives vs. Liberals, Blue Lives vs. Black Lives—and to hold things simply as ideas or issues or topics. And honestly, that probably makes it easier on our consciences, but it is not the way forward. And we, as the church, cannot afford to continue to do that here.

I am sure you have been on a journey of your own as you have navigated the waters of faith's intersection with sexuality and gender identity. Maybe you are at a church where your lead pastor or the elder team feel differently about this conversation than you do.

Maybe you are a part of a denomination that seems to be shifting its perspective in this conversation and you are holding your breath, waiting to see what will happen. Or maybe you just had your very first student come out to you, and in that moment you found that you could not actually say any of the things you thought you might say to them. All of the one-liners and theological "ammunition" you had prepared for your conversation with an LGBTQ student would not come out. I know how you feel.

Over the past few years, my understanding of and insight into this conversation has been challenged and expanded, shaped, and reshaped; and I have grown in ways I never expected. I pray and hope the same for you.

MY JOURNEY

I grew up in what some might call a "hyper-evangelical" setting where the Bible was, and is, the absolute authority on all things. Like many, I learned to toe the party line when it came to the LGBTQ conversation, which was to say, "The Bible clearly condemns homosexuality." Paul says so in Romans 1, 1 Corinthians 6, and 1 Timothy 1. (Plus, there are all those Old Testament verses!) It all seems rather straightforward (no pun intended), right? And though I am a Millennial and statistically our generation is widely affirming of same-sex marriage in our country,[2] while growing up, I never knew anyone who openly identified as gay or lesbian—no friends or fellow students and no family members. There were a few teenagers in my high school who everyone thought were gay; but I never knew for sure. So for many years, this conversation stayed largely in this realm: Here is the topic and here is the correct biblical answer. Admittedly, this was a comfortable place to be because in that church culture, any time you got to feel unequivocally sure of

2. "Changing Attitudes on Gay Marriage: Public Opinion on Gay Marriage," *Pew Research Center: Religion and Public Life* (website), June 26, 2017, http://www.pewforum.org/2016/05/12/changing-attitudes-on-gay-marriage/.

the right biblical teaching, it felt good—righteous even.

So throughout high school and into college, when asked, my answer was clear: "Homosexuality is a sin."

Fast-forward to 2011. My wife worked as a designer for a small independent design firm here in Denver, and her boss was a gay woman who had a wonderful wife. They had two beautiful children, a house, and a dog just like traditional families; and one evening they invited us over for dinner.

Until then, I had never interacted socially with anyone who openly identified as LGBTQ. I simply did not know anyone in that community. At the time, I was part-time staff at DCC; and I knew my "good, Christian answer" in regard to the LGBTQ conversation. But something in me had already begun to shift from understanding Christianity purely as an institutionalized religion that demanded my unwavering loyalty and rightness, to understanding my Christian faith as something I did in following Jesus—and having to reconcile how the idea of "following Jesus" was very different from the faith I was handed growing up. As such, I had no issues at all with my wife working with and for this couple, or even with us being invited over for dinner with their family. So we happily went.

We ate dinner on the patio with their two elementary-aged daughters, who ran around with the dog, laughing and having a great time. All the while, we watched these women parent their children, make us dinner, and help with homework. We had a great time, enjoyed our meal, wrapped up our night, and said our goodbyes. When my wife and I got in our car we reflected on something we found interesting. But first, a little backstory on us...

We both grew up in separated families: My parents divorced when I was in second grade; my wife's, when she was in third grade.

We know what it is like to have bedrooms at both mom's and dad's houses. We know what it is like to spend Thanksgiving with Mom and Christmas with Dad. We know what it's like to grow up with stepparents and stepsiblings; and we have navigated all of the awkward family dynamics that divorce brings with it, both as children and now as adults.

Now, don't get me wrong; we love all our parents and siblings, no matter their titles or biological relationship to us. But when looking at our families and reflecting on our experiences, there is this sense that something just below the surface was "off." Packing bags for the weekend and splitting time between parents is not really the preferred childhood picture. It's supposed to be two parents and their kids at home together, doing the family thing. And since neither my wife nor I had that experience growing up, we have longed for it so much that when we see it in healthy families, it always strikes a chord.

Now, we have seen this beautiful "nuclear" family modeled in many heterosexual relationships over the years; but as we left dinner that night after being with two moms and their children, we sensed in this particular family that something was better than we had imagined. This couple, who supposedly were "not doing family and marriage the right way" had built and possessed something that was better, in many ways, than what we had growing up. Somehow, this thing that had been sold to us as wrong and sinful and "detestable in the eyes of the Lord" did not feel that way in real life.

And at the time, though we may not have believed what they had was as good as having a traditional mom-and-dad combo, it was really close. There was something honest, pure, and sacred about their family; and in that moment, the cognitive dissonance many Christians carry with them around this conversation started to reveal itself to me.

WHAT DRIVES MY VIEW

Fast-forward to 2015. I was now full time at DCC, we had grown to two locations in the city of Denver, and the Supreme Court had just ruled in favor of same-sex marriage. The social and political landscape of our country was shifting; and in the middle of all of this, our staff was asking all sorts of questions. Questions like:

Do we have any openly gay people at DCC?
Would we allow a gay couple to use our chapel for their wedding?
Would we, as pastors, officiate a gay wedding?
Would we be forced to do gay weddings under the new law?
What do we believe about this and do we all feel the same way?

Perhaps you are familiar with these questions and others like them. At the same time, the men and women of our elder team embarked on a journey to discover how DCC would move forward in this changing landscape. What would our "position" be? How would we respond? What did we understand the Bible to say? And did we all, as staff and leadership, understand it in the same way?

Previously we intentionally maintained an ambiguous position, leaving room for speculation and questions around what the leadership of DCC actually believed; but we could no longer hold that position. So our elders spent nearly two years studying Scripture, praying together, challenging one another, hearing from various viewpoints, and listening to those in the LGBTQ community share their stories. Then, in late 2016, each and every elder unanimously supported our direction as a faith community toward full inclusion for LGBTQ people.

DCC purposely chose to use the words "full inclusion" and not "open and affirming," as "open and affirming" can imply that everyone within a community *affirms* LGBTQ relationships. If that is the case, it can make it difficult for anyone who is not affirming to stay because a line has been drawn in the sand. The desire of our elders was to be inclusive of all people with various viewpoints, lest they marginalize those who are not affirming. This direction was affirmed by our friends in the LGBTQ community who encouraged our elder team to leave room for various viewpoints. They did not want those who are not affirming to feel unwelcome in the church.

Did you catch that?

Members of the LGBTQ community did not want those who disagree with them and their relationships to feel the same way some in the church have made them feel. I have learned so much about grace, love, forgiveness and acceptance from my LGBTQ friends and students; and I am grateful for that.

Over that two-year period, our staff and leadership had time and space to process and pray, read and research, and come to a more helpful understanding of our personal positions on same-sex attraction (SSA) and subsequently the LGBTQ conversation. As our executive pastor has pointed out, many people of faith simply adopt a system of belief that has been handed down to them fully formed and often fail to interrogate those beliefs themselves. We were invited to do just that. To challenge and interrogate our beliefs with freedom to learn, study, think, and grow.

And here is the crazy part, if this is not already sounding crazy to you: From the beginning it was made clear that there was not going to be an expectation or parameter on where we needed to land in this conversation. No one in leadership has ever "officially" asked for my position or viewpoint. In fact, our elders are not in agreement on what the biblical implications are regarding the LGBTQ community in our culture today.

You read that correctly: *Some of our elders can and do affirm same-sex relationships, and some of them can't and won't.* If there is a story coming out of DCC in this season—and you can imagine a few have been written online—*this* is the story. A group of men and women came to different conclusions regarding the Bible and still decided to move forward together in a new way, following Jesus. With *hundreds* of denominations in the Christian church in our country—most of them born out of "Oh you do that differently than us? We will go over here"—the fact that no one in leadership has left DCC or their position over this decision is remarkable. To this day, our elder team is still not in a place of full agreement. However, they felt called to transcend their individual viewpoints and seek unity; and this is what they prayed for—that we would experience unity over uniformity. Unity not only with one another, but for us as a full faith community—even in the midst of divergent perspectives.

If Jesus needed to pray for us to be one, just as he and the Father are one (John 17:20-21), then it seems to me that he knew there were going to be lots of things we would disagree on. Honestly, if we were going to start splitting up our churches *any* time we found a "theological disagreement," we wouldn't even get down the alphabetical list to H for "homosexuality" before we walked out the door. You do not have to work at or be a part of a church or community that simply affirms and confirms your previously held beliefs. In fact, you probably shouldn't be. If you agree with everything your lead pastor says, you may have a problem. (And yes, our lead pastor says that... on Sunday mornings.)

So there I was, a young youth pastor, trying to grow a student ministry in the transient, postmodern context of Denver, Colorado, with a leadership team that just dropped one of the biggest church-bombs you can have in our culture today. I was filled with questions:

What did this mean for me?

What did this mean for our youth?

What did this mean for our volunteer leaders?

What did this mean for small group conversations and room assignments at winter retreat?

How were the parents of our students going to react?

How were my parents going to react?

And you may be thinking... *I know! That's why I'm reading this book! Do you have any answers?*

Actually... I do. Sort of. They are more suggestions than answers. I can only tell you what is working for us.

Inclusion: A Matter of Life or Death

I start any practical conversation about interacting with or pastoring LGBTQ students with the reality that teenagers kill themselves every day. Each day in our country there are, on average, over 5,000 suicide attempts made by students grades seven through twelve.[3]

Over 5,000!

These could be students in any one of *our* youth ministries. And we all know LGBTQ students report more bullying, more victimization at school, more frequent feelings of depression and struggles with anxiety. Which raises an important question: *What percentage of that 5,000 identify as LGBTQ?*

> "...The topic of this book is literally life or death for some teens."

With bullying and feelings of depression and anxiety at the top of the list of why teens attempt suicide, it's a safe bet that LGBTQ youth make up a fair amount of these statistics. Which means the topic of this book is literally life or death for some teens.

Life. Or death.

And seemingly, this is supposed to be our wheelhouse as the church, right? Life and death. How to live and breathe and experience freedom and the Good News of Jesus in this life. Along with how to understand and have faith about death and the life to come through Christ in the next. You would think that the church would be the place that was most welcoming to folks who were wrestling with topics as grave as this, but that hasn't been the case. It is amazing that we have mucked this up so badly thus far, and we need to learn from

---

3. "Suicide Statistics," *The Jason Foundation: The Parent Resource Program* (website), August 9, 2017, http://jasonfoundation.com/prp/facts/youth-suicide-statistics/.

our mistakes.

How many times has a student or volunteer told you about something they remember *you* saying, yet you do not remember saying it? It happens all the time because our students, our volunteers, and parents are listening. If you are in a leadership position in your faith community, you have more influence than you may know. So we need to start by being aware of what we are saying—our humor, our sarcasm, and the words we choose to speak. We need to be aware of what articles and blogs we post and "like" on Facebook. We need to be aware, because our students are paying attention and our leaders are watching. How we respond and carry ourselves matters, *especially* to LGBTQ teens—and this is just the tip of the iceberg. If this is, in fact, a life-or-death conversation, then we need to be prepared.

So how do we pastor the LGBTQ youth in our ministry at DCC? I'll give the shortest, most honest answer I have, which may feel confusing at first: *We simply treat LGBTQ students the way we treat any other student.*

Every Student Is Unique

Is there some sort of student ministry Rolodex (wow, that metaphor has some staying power) of stock answers that we give to *all* of our students? Of course not! We know that each time a situation or conversation comes up, our response is going to vary depending on the youth and their context.

Whether their parents are getting divorced or their grandparent has passed away or their girlfriend/boyfriend broke up with them or they didn't make varsity or they are feeling depressed and started cutting or got caught with marijuana... our answers are different because each student's life and situation is different.

This is why we do not have stock, black-and-white answers for every situation. If we did, we wouldn't need this book. We'd have all the answers. But we already pastor each student in our ministry differently, because they are all different kids. This is because at the heart of pastoring is relational engagement. It is about knowing our youth and their circumstances. Knowing their faith backgrounds. Knowing about their families. It is also why we spend lots of time developing a dynamic team of volunteers to engage our students.

We need all kinds of people on our student ministry teams because we have all kinds of students in our ministries, including

> "We simply treat LGBTQ students the way we treat any other student."

LGBTQ youth, whether you know it or not. And we need all kinds of responses and approaches to different situations that our youth are going to face. Which means when asked about our "policy" regarding LGBTQ students, or any student for that matter, there is no way for me to give a singular answer. Here is a real-life example…

We had a student transition from having been assigned female at birth to presenting as male. We have known this teen for a long time. He had gone to camp with us as *she*, and then a few weeks later reentered our ministry as *he*. Which meant we had a couple of practical questions to answer. First, "What should we do about his small group participation?"—which is something typically determined by grade and gender. Second, "What should we do about which gender leader handles his contact work/relational ministry outside of our building?" Given that we have a very strict parameter that our leaders only pursue relationship with students of the same gender, how did we want to proceed?

With our goal and hope being to serve and care for our youth and their families, we are learning that we will not serve them well if we do not first ask what they need. This is true especially in times of crisis, which is how someone coming out—whether as lesbian, gay, bi, transgender, or queer—tends to present itself in the lives of families.

So that's what we did. We first journeyed alongside his parents, helped with counseling referrals, and reassured them that their son was completely welcome and free to be a part of our ministry exactly how he was, no need to change or hide what he was navigating. He was free to participate with and alongside our male students if that was what he wanted. We then asked him how he wanted to be reintroduced to the group. We asked him what would help him feel most comfortable and asked him which leaders he wanted to stay connected to.

If you have interacted with parents of LGBTQ students, you know that they generally feel that the rug has just been pulled out from underneath them, and your simple assurance that their child is welcome, no questions asked, will mean the world. I think this is an incredible opportunity to echo Jesus' invitation of welcoming those who are "tired, worn out, and burned out on religion."[4] To the folks who are heavy-burdened and in need of rest, we get to literally live out the message of Jesus by saying, "You are safe. We are with you. There is no expectation here." And to a parent who doesn't even know which direction is up, this is good news.

Ultimately, through many conversations with this youth and his parents, we decided to move forward by having him jump into a boys small group. If he is going to express his gender as male, then he is welcome to be in a boys small group. But he also decided to keep his relational connection with one of our female leaders, who would continue to be the one who would pursue relationship with him outside of our gatherings because he already had a well-established relationship with her. This was a mutual decision; she knew of his transition from the beginning and wanted to be the one to continue down that road with him.

Now, will this be what we do for *every* transgender youth? Of course not. We have learned there is no one way to do this. We will never be able to accurately predict or forecast what different LGBTQ students will need. This is what I have shared with parents who want to know what our response will be if and when a student comes out in small group or how we are going to handle LGBTQ youth wanting to be in relationship in our community. In order to answer those questions, I need to ask a few of my own.

---

4. This is a paraphrase of Matthew 11 from Eugene Peterson's *The Message* (NavPress, 1993).

In fact, the best policy we have around pastoring LGBTQ youth is learning to ask helpful questions. We work to gather as much information as we can to figure out how we can come alongside the student (and hopefully their parents) to support them. Here are the questions we ask:

How old is the student?

How long have they known they are [insert relevant LGBTQ or SSA identity]?

How are they identifying gender-wise or in regard to their sexuality, and do they know what it means? (Yes, some students are confused.)

How long have they been public and who else knows?

What is their family of origin and how are their parents reacting?

How does the teen feel about it? (guilt? shame? excitement? joy?)

What is the anticipated social "fallout"? (sports, activities, friends/family, etc.)

What is their history in our ministry?/How long have we known them?

What is their connection to our leadership team?

And then we also ask a few questions about their history with anxiety, depression, and life circumstances. You can see the seemingly endless number of variables here.

> "...The best policy we have around pastoring LGBTQ youth is learning to ask helpful questions."

Take for example thirteen-year-old Sarah. She told us that she was a lesbian and had felt that way for the last six months. Her friends at school knew but her parents did not. She knew that being lesbian meant she "liked girls," but she seemed to be using the term "girlfriends" in a way that someone might use it for their platonic female friends. Her parents had been divorced for the past few years, and she was more nervous for her dad to find out than her mom. She had only been a part of our ministry for a few months. Her parents did not come to our church, and she had originally come with a friend. We had been seeing her on a regular basis, but she did not have a go-to leader connection at the time.

Or there was seventeen-year-old Chris, who told us he was gay and had known since he was eight. Both his friends and family knew and were supportive of him. He was nervous to come out at church, but felt it was a safe place to do so. I had known him for a while but never knew this about him. He even had a girlfriend at one point. His mom and dad were a part of our community and wanted to work with our student ministry going forward on how to support Chris and other LGBTQ youth and families. He had a great relationship with his small group leader, and they had a set time to hang on a monthly basis.

I tell you these two stories because they clearly call for very different responses. The point being, there is no one way to pastor youth, LGBTQ or otherwise. And though that might feel like too much ambiguity or like a bit of a non-answer, acknowledging this has been something that has served us very well thus far. And though we only made our decision to move to full inclusion a short time ago, we have been operating our youth ministry like this for years.

The thing about asking questions is that it automatically puts you into a posture of humility and listening. I have never felt there was some sort of silver-bullet answer for all of the problems, questions, or situations that our youth are going to face in this life. In the same way that each of our students is unique, so is every situation. Which means I always need more information. Whether we are journeying with a student who is navigating crippling insecurity around their LGBTQ status or a situation that we as youth workers feel we have navigated hundreds of times before, we are going to need to know the starting point before we can give directions. Even the decision to follow Jesus looks different for each of our youth as they are starting their faith journeys from different places. And I believe the more we can shift gears and get into this sort of mindset, the more equipped and confident we will be to pastor and care for students of the

LGBTQ community.

The Church Has to Be Safe

History will show that today's teenagers have grown up in a world vastly different than the world of the generation before them, which is nothing new. From the Internet and social media to iPhones and Snapchat, their worldview is entirely different. Students are saying, experiencing, and feeling all sorts of things that most Millennials never did, let alone Gen Xers or Boomers. I had a seventh-grade girl at youth group tell me a story that started with the words "I have a friend at school who is trans and…"

She has a friend who is transgender in the seventh grade? I literally (to my knowledge) met my first transgender friend this past year, and I am thirty-two. She is twelve. Our students hold a very different paradigm around this conversation. We hosted a five-week learning group to announce and process with our community our decision to move towards full inclusion, and at that time many of our students did not attend but instead asked, "Why are we still talking about this?" I'm sure you don't need me to tell you, but that gives you a sense of where this generation is at when it comes to the LGBTQ conversation.

> "Do LGBTQ teens feel safe enough in our ministries to come out to us?"

A few years ago, we did a season of small groups on relationships and dating. In one of our high school small groups, a girl said, plain as day, "When I get married one day, to a man or a woman…" When I heard that I was, honestly, pretty surprised. That is a very different expectation than I had for my future spouse. But students who are experiencing SSA or who identify as LGBTQ need a place to be able to say these things.

Which raises an important question: "Do LGBTQ teens feel safe enough in our ministries to come out to us?" If you have never had a student in your ministry come out as LGBTQ, the answer to that question might be no.

As we think about how we will respond to the LGBTQ conversation and what policies we will put in place around pastoring LGBTQ students, we must start with the idea that the church—specifically, our student ministries—should be a safe place for LGBTQ teenagers to have these conversations and ask these questions. Take it a step further; the church needs to be the *safest* place for teens—*all* teens, regardless of sexual orientation or gender identity—to come process and figure out life.

Our youth need a place to ask questions, to express doubt. To wrestle with life, and their sexuality, and their parents' divorce, and high school drama and everything else that is getting thrown their way. If we are not creating space where youth feel safe enough to be open, honest, and vulnerable about the realities of their lives, then we might as well close up shop.

Those who find the church to be unsafe often run away to experience something different. Far too many say, "If this is what Jesus is all about, then I don't want anything to do with him." And few run out of the doors of one church and into another. To put it another way, nobody runs out of a burning building—a place that has caused them pain and hurt—looking for safety and shelter, only to run across the street into another burning building. In those moments all churches are guilty by association.

I have heard *so* many stories of people who admittedly and intentionally swung the pendulum the other direction, away from their parents' faith, from the morals of the church, and who ended up getting hurt and doing terrible damage to their lives—not because of their sexual orientation or gender identity but because they didn't have any place to belong or feel safe.

Part of what was so upsetting about the shooting at Pulse nightclub in Orlando was the reality that it took place in what was supposed to be a safe place. With few places left to turn, dance clubs like Pulse have become safe havens for the LGBTQ community. In a world where LGBTQ folks cannot be honest or real in many environments, let alone in church, where are they supposed to go? They end up creating their own communities looking for the same thing we all are. LGBTQ individuals want to love and be loved. That this terrible violence took place in one of the few safe spaces for the LGBTQ community should upset us all. We must be willing to recognize we literally and figuratively have played a role in chasing LGBTQ people away from the church. We must reconcile that.

I am sure we can all agree that our ministries have to be a safe place for students, but they need to be an even

"Our youth need a place to ask questions, to express doubt."

safer place for LGBTQ teens. This is true regardless of where we land in the theological conversation. Maybe you are in a place where you do not think you will be able to affirm LGBTQ relationships. Okay. Maybe you *can* affirm LGBTQ relationships. Okay. Either way, if we really want to care for LGBTQ youth, making our student ministries the safest place for them to talk, process, and be real is the first step.

Holding the Tension

What has been interesting about the journey at DCC since becoming an "inclusive" community, is it means we have parents and families on both sides of the conversation. And despite what some might have you believe, the church's position on the matter isn't clear cut; and there are lots of perspectives in the LGBTQ conversation. Which means, even if your church's public position on the matter is not the same as DCC's, it is very likely you have folks in your community— students, parents, and families—who hold different perspectives and opinions. I have had meetings with different sets of parents in the same week, where I show up, sit down, and they ask me the same question: "In light of DCC's recent decision, how is this going to affect the youth ministry?"

What's fun is that some of those parents are affirming of the LGBTQ community and some are not, which means I am being asked the same question from different perspectives from people who are hoping for very *different* responses. The affirming parents, some of which are parents of LGBTQ teens, want to know what we are going to do to implement, encourage, and further the reality of being an inclusive community.

While parents on the other side, who are concerned their biblical understanding of marriage and homosexuality is not being echoed and upheld by the folks who have influence in the lives of their impressionable teens, also want to know how our ministry is going to look moving forward.

No matter our personal theological positions, no matter our church's official stance, we need to have an answer to these questions; and at DCC our answer is straightforward.

Before coming out as inclusive, we were not pushing some sort of "straight agenda," encouraging students towards heterosexual interactions and relationships. In the same way, we are not now pushing some sort of "LGBTQ agenda," where we are encouraging or offering up the idea of identifying as LGBTQ as the new way forward. Now, just as before, our main concern is helping youth understand that their sole (soul) identity comes from being an image bearer, a beloved child of God. That they were beautifully and wonderfully made, wired for relationship with the Father and other humans in community, and that they need people in their lives to support them.

No human relationship, gay or straight, will ever give any of us our true sense of value, worth, or identity in this world. That understanding of identity only comes from one place. We can and will speak into the moments of realization and discovery around students' sexuality, attraction, and relationships; but we will do so on an individual basis. As I have said, we must pastor each of our youth differently, according to their needs and circumstances. But there are constants for us.

We maintain a very conservative sexual ethic at DCC. We believe in committed, consensual, long-term, monogamous, married relationships. And that any expression of sexuality should be expressed in that context. We believe pornography kills love.[5]

---

5. If you don't know about fightthenewdrug.org, now you do.

We believe any expression of sexuality that exploits or manipulates another person is outside of God's design for human relationship. And we believe that promiscuity and infidelity are harmful to everyone. But these boundaries, these parameters have to be communicated in trusting, relational contexts if we want them to be received. And to do that, I need more information about who I am talking to.

GETTING PRACTICAL

In my experience, creating a trusting, relational context for all students takes intentionality and thoughtfulness. It requires constantly re-examining the "way we've always done it" and imagining how it can be better. Here is what we are learning…

Respond more often with questions. It's tempting to believe we are supposed to have all the answers. We are professional Christians, right? It's hard to imagine how we landed there given that we follow the guy who answered almost every question with more questions. What if we took Jesus' approach and applied it to our pastoral work and our small group leader training? We should always ask more questions and stop trying to give black-and-white answers, contributing to a culture where students learn there is "only one way to think around here." Youth must know and believe any idea, question, or feeling is welcome if we actually want to get to the real stuff of their lives. I consider it a huge testament to our ministry that so many teens have felt comfortable enough to come out in our small group settings, and I attribute that to the culture of openness we have created.

Give constructive advice. When you were in middle school and high school, and someone in a position of authority told you, "Don't do_____!" or "Stop that!" did it ever keep you from doing the exact thing they told you not to do? That's the fun of being a teenager. Which means we have to decide if we want the advice and insight we give our students to go in one ear and out the other, or if we want it to matter. If we want it to matter, we need to figure out how to deliver it in a way that might stick. In my experience, adolescents do not want to be told what to do. For teens, everyone in their lives is doing that already—mom, dad, stepparents, siblings, teachers, coaches, principals, and hall monitors. Even our culture and social media are telling them who to be and how to act.

Do you want to end up at the bottom of a long list of people who talk *at* our youth? I don't. I want to be at the top of the list of people who students know love and care for them and just want what is best for them. This means I'm not going to tell them what to do or how to live their lives every chance I get. My plan is to listen, ask good questions, offer suggestions, present multiple options and perspectives, and give our teens an opportunity to figure it out for themselves. Once they think it's their idea, they will like it way more anyway. (I call it inception.)

Begin including LGBTQ leaders in your youth ministry. Say you were going to open a restaurant, and you happened to have the best physical space and location in town. And you had the best chef, menu, and food to go with it. Slam dunk, right? Having worked in a restaurant for nearly a decade and eaten in restaurants for most of my life, I can tell you unequivocally that the most important part of a restaurant experience is the staff. How many times have a you had a great meal, only to have it ruined by a grumpy server? Plenty, I'm sure. More than good food, the attitude and presence of the restaurant staff can make or break any experience.

In the same way, the most important asset of our youth ministry is our volunteer leadership team. The way I see it, you can have the coolest building, the biggest youth ministry budget, the most hip and relevant youth pastor ever... but if you don't have an incredible group of people able and willing to invest in your youth, you'd have nothing. You'd be a Michelin-star restaurant with no one to run the dining room. Our volunteers are the folks who do the long, hard work of investing in and connecting with our students. And the benefit of all these leaders and relationships is that when a teen goes through a breakup or has their parents get divorced or a grandparent pass away, *someone* on the team can say, "I know exactly how you feel because I have been there."

So the question is, if we are really going to serve and pastor our LGBTQ youth well, do we have anyone on our team who can say, "I've been there"? Maybe your church isn't affirming. Maybe your church leadership won't permit an LGBTQ individual to volunteer. I understand that. All I know is that it has become a huge value for us to have older LGBTQ Christians who are able to speak to the intricacies of coming out and who can navigate those waters with teens; and my dream is that the LGBTQ student leaders doing this work with their younger peers in our ministry right now will be joined by *adult* LGBTQ leaders in the near future. It's important; and if we want our LGBTQ youth to have the same experience as our other youth, we need to get Christian LGBTQ leaders in the game.

Teach teenagers *how* to think. Lastly, do we want to simply give someone a fish or do we want to teach that person how to fish? How can we help our students learn how to think instead of just teaching them *what* to think?

I remember taking math in high school and getting marked down for not showing my work. I was good at math and could do most of it in my head. Turns out,

> "...If we want our LGBTQ youth to have the same experience as our other youth, we need to get Christian LGBTQ leaders in the game."

being able to prove that you understand what you did is *as* important as getting the right answer. What if our youth actually felt that way about their faith? What if our students were invited into the wide and expansive joy of following Jesus, and what if they knew how they got there? What if they knew what they believed and why they believed it? What if we started inviting them into something that actually looked like "life to the full" and not just a static set of propositions to adhere to? If we can do that, I believe our youth will in fact know how to fish.

FINAL THOUGHTS

There is no one way to pastor LGBTQ teenagers, and I cannot possibly tell you how to pastor in your context. I simply hope and pray that when all is said and done, when the history books go to print, or when someone picks this book up years from now we will have gotten some things right. We have a long way to go, but I believe we can do it. The more I learn about Jesus and the more I orient my faith and ministry around his radically inclusive love, the more I realize how *good* the Good News actually is. When we begin to figure that out for ourselves, we will want to share it even more with as many youth as possible, especially those who have long been told that the Good News is not for them.

Recently, I told my mom the story about meeting Doug and Daisy that first Sunday they showed up at DCC. I told her how I'd apologized for how other churches might have made Daisy feel when I told her how happy I was she was there. That's when my mom pointed out that Daisy will probably remember my response to her forever. My mom said, "In that moment, you were not responding as Nick Elio, or even as a pastor at Denver Community Church. You were responding as *the* church."

Her insight helped me see how we respond to the next student we interact with—straight, gay, bi, cisgender, trans, queer, or questioning—matters. And it may be a matter of life or death. May our responses by filled with the grace and peace and inclusive love of Jesus.

RESPONSE

BY SHELLEY DONALDSON

Clearly, Nick and his church community are trying to live into that radical welcome that Jesus calls for. *Yes.* This is a step in the right direction. There is something to be said for treating LGBTQ youth just like any other youth. When I came out as a young adult, I wanted to be treated like any other young adult. Nothing in me had changed; I was simply living into who I was created to be. And teenagers are similar: They want to be treated like everyone else. Knowing people and being in relationships with one another is important. That's how our hearts change. But being a welcoming church and creating a table of tolerance, while important, is not enough.

As Christians, we are called to act. We are called to be radical in so many ways. And being a welcoming church and truly living into the welcome all people, regardless of where you stand on an issue, is definitely part of being that radical church. I can only imagine the pushback from other churches that DCC, Nick's church, might have gotten as they shifted toward their current perspective. But we can't stop there.

It's a perspective that, to me, is a stance of tolerance. It is a start to that radical welcome, but I don't believe it's enough.

One thing I see as lacking here is an addressing of the harm that has been done to LGBTQ people by the church and actively doing more to change that. Adding more chairs to the table won't cut it. All that does is tell LGBTQ youth, "Come to our table. There are still people here who think you are sinful and don't agree with your sexuality. But you are welcome to be here anyway." And, in light of that, we have to ask the question: *Can a church be truly welcoming without a theology change?* Without a full agreement toward affirmation in this area, a church would still ostensibly operate in a heteronormative way that doesn't make space for seeing the Bible from the lens of an LGBTQ person. Would such a church still use male-only pronouns for God, for example?

A welcome like that could come off as mere lip service.

What this does is set up an environment of tolerance. Tolerance is fine, until it's not. Tolerance is a halfway mark, not true welcome. For example, I can tolerate a crying child on an airplane because I don't have to interact with the child. Eventually I'll get off the plane and won't have to see the child again. I am under no obligation to engage with this child, we are simply there for an end goal: to get from Point A to Point B. That should not be the case with the church.

As faithful Christians, we cannot simply tolerate one another as we sit in a service and then go our separate ways without actually knowing and fully loving each other. We have to actually be engaged with and experience empathy for one another, especially for those in the minority. In this case, that's the LGBTQ community. And that is hard. Because giving up some tightly held power as a dominant voice in the church or society is hard. When power is given away, it may feel like oppression. And no one willingly wants to feel as though they have less power. A stance that boils down to tolerance—even well-meaning tolerance—does not fully affirm who these LGBTQ youth are and does nothing to empower them. It's difficult to see how merely having the affirmation of a *portion* of a church is enough. Being tolerated is not being welcomed.

All this being said, Nick is absolutely right. It is important to have LGBTQ mentors and volunteers within the church and for that youth program. But we should not be mistaken for guinea pigs. It is all too common for anyone in a minority position. LGBTQ adults are not the only ones who can and should minister to LGBTQ youth, and we can't teach heterosexual youth leaders how to do it either. Those in ministry must go further by doing things like changing our language and asking the question, "How does an LGBTQ youth see this Scripture?" I believe that unless we are willing to really change who we are as a church, welcoming people to the table is not enough.

As a Presbyterian, I believe in holding tension; but I also believe in changing hearts. Isn't that what we are called to do as followers of Christ? So, welcome can't just be a sign on the door or a seat at the table; it must be the *action of change* toward full inclusion and affirmation of LGBTQ individuals in every aspect of the church and church leadership and not just conversation and understanding between people with different viewpoints. We need hearts to change, not the size of the table.

VIEW 3: BELONGING AND TRANSFORMATION

BY ERIC WOODS

"So, what does the church think of gay people?" These were the first words she spoke to me on her first day at chapel. It was a question I had thought about... but not thought enough about to answer her with care and honesty.

It was her first day participating in our ministry, and I had already heard about her, before she'd even asked that question. New to our community, it was no secret that this middle school girl was struggling with her sexual identity.

I had been caught off guard with questions from middle schoolers before—questions like "Why did God let my parents get a divorce?" and "How do we know the Bible is true?" and "What's for snack?" But this question was different. Clearly not intended to be a trap, this young person genuinely wanted to know if there was a place for her in the church and, in particular, in *our* ministry.

Of course, it was at that moment I realized that the song that just started playing on the Pandora pre-service playlist was likely to get me fired if anyone else noticed… and remembered we still had to finish getting the slides ready for worship.

It was a question, I told her, that would have to wait for another time. "But for now, you should know that you are absolutely welcome here."

I could see a bit of relief in her expression; and she and her friend, who was clearly there for moral support, went and found seats.

Later that day I came back to her question, mulling over and over in my mind what the people in the churches I was most familiar with did think about gay people—or, in more general terms, any individuals who identify as part of the LGBTQ community. And, having spent most of my life and ministry in the most conservative churches and Christian circles, the answers I was coming up with weren't exactly things that would make for a hopeful response to a searching teenager.

I had heard respected Christian leaders talk about the "gay agenda" which was "threatening our culture and way of life."

I had heard pastors and conference speakers offer pat answers for why some people "ended up" gay (or bisexual or transgender, etc.), and ideas for how they could be "fixed."

I had known older people in the church who were not afraid to say that "gays shouldn't be coming to church" and certainly weren't welcome to take communion or serve in any capacity.

And I'd had parents of students check in with me to make sure that certain teens—gay teens, specifically—from school weren't coming to youth group or planning to sleep in the same room as their kids at camp.

Sure, I had an idea what the conservative churches I was most familiar with thought of LGBTQ people, and I certainly wasn't going to say it out loud. But I also knew that attitudes and perceptions about being gay and how LGBTQ individuals fit into the church have begun to shift, even among the most conservative.

Nevertheless, I knew that I had one chance to respond to this teen. I knew that my words could serve to further erode the trust she had in the church or to, at a minimum, extend the opportunity I had for influence in her life.

WHAT DRIVES MY VIEW, PT. 1

"Do you believe kids can change?"

It was the fundamental question I was asked in the interview for my current ministry position. I serve as the pastor to residents and staff at a nonprofit social service agency that provides residential care and community-based services for youth and families in crisis. It's also the question *every* candidate for employment is asked. At the core, the agency wants to know that their employees believe that the youth who come to us with the most traumatic hurts and deepest secrets really do have a chance for life change.

Most people answer something like "absolutely" or "for sure" and follow it up with why—usually having something to do with the fact that they've experienced significant transformation and healing personally or have seen it in people they care for deeply.

I answered yes too, but perhaps with a slightly different reason. I believe young people can change because I believe God changes young people. Of course, he changes adults too. It is, in fact, the foundational premise of my philosophy of ministry. Whether we're at rock bottom or at least seem to have it all together, God wants to bring transformation, healing, and change. And he can. And he does. I think I first realized this during my first couple of years in campus ministry.

Transformation: The Possibility of Change
College students tend to be passionate people, and the ones I worked with were passionate about reaching their fellow students. They did

everything they could to turn their attention away from the parties and alcohol. They did things like pass out thousands of free hot dogs to passersby on the road to the fraternity and sorority houses. They offered free rides home, no questions asked, first on the strip at Panama City Beach during spring break, then on the streets of their own campus on St. Patrick's Day. They camped out on the edge of campus for sixty-eight hours, reading the Bible out loud from cover to cover in a tent without stopping—all for the chance to connect with one of their peers and have an opportunity to see God change a life.

And they did. Josh, for example, was one of the guys they met in a van in Panama City Beach. His name kept popping up on the prayer board back at headquarters because there seemed to be some breakthrough happening in his life. Josh was ready for change, and he wasn't getting out of that van until it had taken hold.

Until that point, Josh's life had been filled with—or even defined by— his sexual immorality, drunkenness, and all kinds of anger, slander, and selfishness.

It didn't happen all at once in that van on the strip in Panama City Beach, but slowly over time we witnessed Josh's life changing. The things that had defined him were falling away, and Josh was becoming someone new. Those of us who met Josh that first day and were now witnesses to this transformation couldn't help but think of what Paul said when he saw the same sort of transformation in the lives of the Corinthians.

In 1 Corinthians 6:11, he wrote, "And that is what some of you were. But you were washed, you were sanctified, you were justified in the name of the Lord Jesus Christ and by the Spirit of our God."

And that is what some of you were.

Transformation is true and real and possible, no matter what has defined a person's past.

In my current ministry, I see it so plainly. Many of the middle and high school students I serve have been physically, emotionally, and sexually abused. When they look in the mirror, they see someone hurt and broken. It's what defines them.

Others have been adjudicated for theft, assault, and criminal sexual conduct. They have been told over and again that they are bad or worthless... or worse. It's what defines them.

Every youth in my ministry sees or has seen themselves this way. It's often the biggest hurdle they have to overcome; and, as their pastor, my job is to help them see that while these things may define their past, they don't define who they are. The God we serve is a God of healing, hope, and transformation.[1] It's a truth no one could argue with.

> "Transformation is true and real and possible, no matter what has defined a person's past."

And when I look into the eyes of my youth—whether they are wrestling with self-worth because of past abuse, or shame due to their past behaviors, or their own sexual identity and behavior—I believe the same for each of them: that God is a God of healing, hope, and transformation.

Belonging: Everyone Is Welcome

So how did I answer that young lady with the striking question? I didn't. Well, at least not in so many words. I decided early on I wasn't going to make a big deal about her sexuality. I wasn't going to talk about it any more than I talked about anyone else's struggle. And I decided I wasn't going to let it come between her and participation in our ministry.

---

1. Many of the organizations that provide the kinds of services we do for youth refer to themselves as "treatment centers" because of the wide range of trauma, suffering, and addictions youth come to us with. And, while we do use the word *treatment*, we have often preferred the word *healing*. We call ourselves a "healing center" and focus on giving young people a safe place to hurt and a safe place to heal.

Instead, I've been consistent about showing her that she belongs in our ministry, that she matters to God, and that she has something to contribute.

She fully expected me to make a big deal about her sexuality. She expected me to reject her like so many churches had before. She expected me to judge her. She expected me to have pat answers. She expected a fight with her new pastor.

Instead, she got a welcome—a consistent welcome. She got a welcome just the same as every other broken life that walks into our chapel. She got a smile, a pat on the back and a side hug. And now, she gets an opportunity to ask and answer questions. She gets to hear week after week about a God who loves her from a ministry that embraces her in all of her brokenness and hurt, just like any other teen.

Several weeks after she joined our community, she approached me with another question that caught me off guard. Again, she had a friend by her side for moral support. "If I wanted to help other students get to know Jesus," she asked, "how would I do that? What could I do?"

She probably saw my jaw fall open, but I gained my composure quickly. Like a good youth pastor, I followed it up with another question, asking her why in the world she would want to do that. And she began to tell me about how God was changing her life: her attitudes, the way she thought about herself, and how she interacted with others.

"Start with that," I told her. "Tell them about how God is changing your life."

So she has. I've heard her talk about the changes he is bringing about in her, and I know she's learning to love more and more the God of healing, hope, and transformation that she is getting to know in our ministry.

I'm not sure I'll ever see healing in her life in terms of her sexuality, but I'm confident I'm seeing healing in her life in so many other ways. And I'm confident that God can bring *complete* healing and restoration in her life in his time.

Hope for Healing

For the most part, the boot camps and therapeutic programs designed to "correct" gender identity and homosexuality—as it is still widely known in the church—have been marginalized, pushed to the fringes. What was once accepted practice among evangelicals is unheard of today. But the core belief that God can and will provide healing in this area remains.

I believe God can heal a person's sexuality. I haven't seen it, but I also haven't seen God heal a paraplegic or restore a blind person's sight. And yet I believe he could do both.

Mark was a high school student when I met him. During college I worked as an IT technician in the local schools, and one of my jobs was to assess needs and provide assistive technology for students with physical disabilities. And, since Mark had been completely blind since birth, his file landed on my desk.

In the 1990s, it was a complicated process to make a computer talk out loud and read or describe what popped up on the screen. The six-button Braille-n-Speak that Mark carried with him everywhere on a strap around his neck did a lot, but nothing in comparison to what I believed a computer could do for him.

> "But the core belief that God can and will provide healing in this area remains. I believe God can heal a person's sexuality."

During our times together, I asked Mark a lot of questions. He was mature for a tenth grader, smart, and a voracious reader. The one book Mark owned in Braille was the Bible—a multi-volume set which showed signs of wear from the repeated reading of his fingertips.

I asked him about his hopes for the future. He wanted to be a preacher.

I asked him how he learned to play the guitar and piano. "By ear," he told me, joking that he still couldn't sight-read the music they handed him in band class.

And I asked him if he ever wished he could see or dreamed that he could. "I don't believe God intended for me to be blind," he told me. "But for now, this is part of who I am."

He told me about how he believed God could heal his sight and knew that it wasn't likely it would happen before he reached heaven.

Mark was the first person to introduce me to the idea of person-first speech. He was, after all, a student, a son, a musician, a Christ-follower, and a friend—among other things—who happened to be blind… not "a blind person." Sure, blindness was a part of his identity, but it wasn't who he was at his core.

In ministry with youth who identify as being gay, bisexual, transgender, or questioning, I try to see them the way I learned to see Mark. I see them as people first. I see them as students who are trying, some of them harder than others, to finish their homework before their favorite shows come on. I see them as athletes and musicians. I see them as young people doing their best to follow Christ with the wisdom they have. And I see them as friends.

And I also see them as people who struggle with an identity that the culture says is "exactly the way God made them" and perhaps their church says is "not what God intends."

But I never lead with that.

MY JOURNEY

I think the right-leaning, conservative end of Christianity has taken a bad rap for being too quick to point out what's wrong with the world, what's wrong with the culture, and what's wrong with teenagers these days. I certainly grew up learning about the things I should avoid in youth group and Sunday school—things like secular music and rated-R movies that weren't already edited for television and, of course, people who were gay or anything else other than cisgender[2] and straight.

There seemed to be a growing divide between people in my life who knew people who were openly gay (and actually liked them) and the people I knew in church who couldn't find a positive thing to think or say about people in the LGBTQ community.

Living most of my life in small towns and rural areas, I honestly didn't have much exposure to the LGBTQ community. There was a person here or there I'd met and the occasional—albeit increasingly familiar—TV sitcom character. But I didn't really know anyone who was gay.

When I did finally get to know some youth involved in my ministry who identified as gay and transgender and who were questioning their sexual identities, I realized something that kind of surprised me. I actually enjoy them. I enjoy their honesty. I enjoy their spunkiness. I enjoy their willingness to take risks. I enjoy their genuine curiosity.

---

2. *Cisgender* is a term that describes a person who identifies with the gender assigned to them at birth. (See the glossary on page 135 for more.)

WHAT DRIVES MY VIEW, PT. 2

In fact, there were a lot of things about the people I was getting to know who were part of the LGBTQ community that I liked, that were good, and that reflected the character and nature of God in them. And, as their pastor, I was faced with a choice: I could focus on the particular issue in their lives that seemed to be farthest from my doctrine and practice, or I could focus on the many things that seemed most consistent.

When one student expected me to reject her because of her sexuality, instead I affirmed her consistent participation in our ministry's programs. When another held back at first, not eager to engage with me or other teens, I affirmed him for his daily Bible reading and study—something, by the way, most other youth weren't doing.

Affirming What You Can
Affirming the positive things I see in students doesn't mean I approve of or endorse their sexual behaviors. It doesn't mean I overlook or wink at what I believe to be sinful. It simply affirms what is good and right.

As I write this, I have a nineteen-month-old foster child in my home. He is fast closing in on the phase of life many call the terrible twos. He's not terrible, but he certainly is good at testing my limits. It's the reason we've installed baby gates, magnetic cabinet door latches, and those annoying little plastic plug covers that you have to pry off with a metal screwdriver when you want to plug in the vacuum cleaner.

The gates and latches aren't there because he doesn't know the stove is hot or the knives are a no-no. He clearly knows. In fact, if I leave one of the gates open, he parades around the kitchen pulling open the knife drawer while he shouts "no" and reaching for the stove while he says "hot." He knows; he just does it anyway.

Gates and latches are really there so I don't have to be the bad guy all the time. Instead of hearing me say "hot" or "no" all the time, he hears me clap and cheer when he drops his toys in the bin. He hears me praise him when he does the right things, and the gates and latches are just boundaries to make doing the right things easier.

I'm a much happier person—and better youth pastor—when I'm affirming my students for the good things I see than when I'm scolding them for the things I don't like.

I did basically the same thing when I worked as a camp director at a large Christian camp. I was tired of listening to the lifeguards at the boating area shout at the campers in canoes to not go near the blobs or not go under the zipline. I mean, this was camp; it was supposed to be fun. And, instead, there was a lot of yelling.

That all ended the day I finally splurged and bought a couple hundred feet of floating rope with buoys to mark off the edge of the canoeing area. Yup. The yelling stopped, and canoeing and blobbing (and lifeguarding) became a lot more fun.

Ministry is a lot more fun when we focus on affirming our youth for the good things we see and eliminate the yelling. Our students will find we're much more enjoyable to be around, and maybe they'll feel loved and stick around long enough to hear about a God who loves them too.

It just seems that for too long our "hating the sin" has been louder than our "loving the sinner." And while the idea that we can love the sinner but hate the sin may work for things like murder or rape, I'm finding that it just doesn't work when I'm ministering to an LGBTQ youth.

A Safe Place

Conservative Christians may be the only people left in America who still think it's possible to love the sinner but hate the sin. In my conversations with teenagers, I'm finding that they are increasingly committed to the idea that their sexuality is not about their gender or what they do in bed or who they choose to love but who they are.

When a church or youth pastor says, "Homosexuality is wrong," they hear, "I am wrong."

When someone says, "Homosexuality is sin," they hear, "I am bad."

When someone talks about gender identity as if it were a threat to their way of life, they feel the full weight of rejection.

If we are truly going to love the sinner while hating the sin, we have to change our language.

Instead of loving the sinner, let's love *the person*. Don't we all have a root of sin in our lives anyway? So why, when it comes to LGBTQ people, do we specifically underline the word *sinner*?

The youth I know who are gay, bi, trans, queer, or questioning need more than anyone else to know that they are loved. They have already known rejection by people who should love them.

So, even though we may not agree with their sexual behaviors or what many in the church would call lifestyle choices, we can still offer love and extend grace.

Ultimately, I believe that God's first priority is not our sexual or gender identity. His first priority is our spiritual identity. He wants us to know that we are his, that we are loved, and that we are being made and remade every day—as 2 Corinthians 3:18 says—to more accurately reflect his glory.

Our youth need to know that their primary identity is not found in their sexuality or their gender, in what they've done or what's been done to them, but in whose they are. As their pastors and youth leaders, we must point them first to Christ and allow him to do his work of transformation in them.

The reality is that we may only have one chance with a student to point them to this truth. We may only have one opportunity to minister to them, one opportunity to make them feel welcome in the church and in our ministries, one opportunity for them to feel like the church really could be a place for them to connect, learn, and grow.

At the Catalyst West Conference in 2015, Pastor Andy Stanley acknowledged the tension that exists in this realm, calling the church to be a safe and welcoming place for students, regardless of our position on these topics. "We just need to decide," he said, "regardless of what you think about this topic—no more students are going to feel like they have to leave the local church because they're same-sex attracted or because they're gay."[3]

> "Our youth need to know that their primary identity is not found in their sexuality or their gender, in what they've done or what's been done to them, but in whose they are."

We've already agreed that the church should be a safe place for students to talk about their parents' divorce—it was for me. We've already decided that it's okay for the church to be a safe space for teens to wrestle with issues of faith and doubt. And if the church can be a safe place for students to discuss and even disagree about these issues, then it can certainly be a safe place for students to be when they're not sure what to think about sexuality.

GETTING PRACTICAL

In middle school I was pretty much always right. At least I thought I was.

I was right about the math problem, right about the grammatical structure of my seventh-grade essays, and right about almost

---

3. Michael Gryboski, "Andy Stanley: Church Should Be the 'Safest Place on the Planet' for Gay Youth," *The Christian Post* (online), April 18, 2015: http://www.christianpost.com/news/andy-stanley-churches-should-be-safest-place-on-the-planet-for-gay-youth-137739/.

everything Christian. I even wore a t-shirt that quoted Psalm 14:1: "The fool says in his heart, 'There is no God.'" The emphasis was on *fool* because, I figured, anyone who disagreed with me (and God), must be a fool.

I think it finally took something like a punch in the gut just outside the first-floor science room to help me realize that being right wasn't winning me any friends. Unfortunately, it took me more than a few more grades to actually start treating people differently. And I wish I could say that was the last time I got punched.

It took at least a couple of years in youth ministry to learn the same lesson: that maybe being pastoral was less about being right and more about creating a safe place for youth to belong, and a safe place for them to grow and learn. And creating that kind of space for teens who identify as gay, bisexual, transgender, queer, or questioning may require some attitude changes and new practices.

Here are a few of the things I've learned:

Be pastoral. It was at one of my own kids' horse shows that I met Big Jim. I was sitting on the end of the bleachers, and he pulled up next to me in one of those tricked out side-by-side off-roading things. The first few words out of his mouth I can't repeat, but they included offensive racial slurs and phrases that would make you blush. He was a big guy, apparently a retired excavator, and was there to watch his grandkids ride horses.

We chitchatted a bit about horses and family, though it felt kind of awkward for me. He told me an off-color joke that only he laughed at. And it was at about that time that his daughter walked up. I knew her well, but hadn't associated the two of them. "I see you met Pastor Eric," she said.

His mouth gaped open. He looked at me in surprise. "Gosh," he said, "if I'd have known you were a preacher, I wouldn't have said half those things."

By my estimation, it would have been closer to seventy percent of the things he said. (And, by the way, he didn't say "gosh.")

But, I guess, Big Jim decided he liked me. I was the first pastor he had ever met, he told me, who didn't try to change him or scold him for using bad language. Of course, I was hopeful for change in Big Jim's life (and I still am); but I knew that pushing him away wasn't going to help bring about that change. I knew that for Big Jim to experience spiritual transformation, he was going to have to spend time around guys like me: pastors who didn't flinch when he cursed and who seemed genuinely interested in his horses, his big hat, and his side-by-side off-roading thing.

> "...We must fight to not let the issue of sexuality preclude all the other issues in these students' lives."

So, I decided I was going to be around Big Jim every chance I got; and when I was, I was going to be pastoral. I would listen, the same as I'd listen to any person in my church or youth group. I would speak truth when I had the opportunity; and I would begin to nudge him, ever so gently, in the right direction.

And, over time, I noticed that Big Jim started to act differently—at least when I was around—and I considered that a step in the right direction.

I know the same is true of the LGBTQ youth in my ministry. They need me to be there, sitting next to them on the bleachers, listening to their war stories and crazy ideas the same way I listen to anyone else's.

They need me to be there to work through their issues of faith and doubt, their disagreements with their parents, and their friendship troubles—the same as any other students.

And the caution that must be raised is that we must fight to not let the issue of sexuality preclude all the other issues in these students' lives. It would be unfair to suggest that sexual healing has to be first in line. Instead, we have to be willing to allow for the possibility that spiritual growth may in fact be a precursor to healing and transformation in terms of sexuality. We have to be willing to dig into messy relationship struggles, difficult family dynamics, and a whole host of other "ordinary" teenage issues first.

Sure, some of their issues may be slightly different than other teenagers, but they still need someone to talk to about them. And when they talk, when they open up and share about their deepest struggles, I listen. When I have the opportunity, I speak gentle words of truth; and little by little, over time, I nudge them in the direction of wholeness and healing.

Be willing to learn. I feel like I handled those first moments with Big Jim on the bleachers pretty well. But I still think back to the day that new student asked about what the church thought of gay people and feel like I missed an opportunity. I missed an opportunity to connect. And I missed an opportunity to relate in a thoughtful way to her struggle—largely, I think, because I didn't know much about her struggle or the struggles of other LGBTQ teenagers.

I knew about the "gay agenda," and I knew a little about the issues of marriage equality which have now become a topic of national conversation and controversy. But I didn't know anything about what an LGBTQ teenager really thought, felt, or experienced on a daily basis.

In general, I've always found it fairly easy to respond confidently to questions I don't really have an answer to. I learned during a mission trip to the Dominican Republic, when our host suddenly had to fly home to the States for a family emergency, that the students getting off the plane at Santiago's international airport needed me—a guy who had only spend a few more hours in the country than they had—to be confident and knowledgeable in order to help them feel safe.

Fortunately, I was quick on my feet to listen as my host drove me through town to the PriceSmart store (the Caribbean version of Sam's Club) and was later able to respond to our students' questions about the geography and culture by repeating things I had heard only an hour before. That group of students developed a quick trust in me; but really, I was making it up as I went.

"Ask me anything," I told them when they climbed on to the bus. "If I don't know the answer, I'll make one up on the spot." I chuckled as I said it; but really, I was only half joking.

However, this doesn't work with our LGBTQ youth. And I've found that more important than being able to have an answer or verse on the spot is my ability to ask good questions and genuinely learn from those I often don't understand well. After all, the best source of information about the needs and struggles of LGBTQ students is not prime-time television, it's LGBTQ students.

So, I've started answering questions with more questions—questions I really want to know the answer to. I ask things like "What do *you* think the church thinks about the LGBTQ community?" and "What is it like to visit a church, go to a new school, or go to your aunt's house for a holiday meal, when you identify as part of the LGBTQ community?"

And the answers are often different from one teenager to the next.

In my current ministry, I have the opportunity to work with students from almost every county in our state. They come from urban centers, rich suburbs, and small rural communities. Their experiences are as different as they come. But each one's experience informs my approach and response.

> "...The best source of information about the needs and struggles of LGBTQ students is not prime-time television, it's LGBTQ students."

Did your last church allow bullying at youth group to make you so uncomfortable that you finally left? We will fight to protect you from that here, being especially sensitive to give other youth a safe place to express concerns and ask questions, but not allow for intimidation.

Have your extended family members disowned you? We'll make sure to connect you with a thoughtful older adult who can mentor you, stepping in to teach you how to fish, how to bake chocolate chip cookies that are still gooey in the middle, how to build a bird house or hem your pants, or how to buy a used car you won't regret.

I want to be knowledgeable, not just about what the letters LGBT and Q stand for but what my LGBTQ students really need to be able to grow in their relationships with Jesus and be emotionally and relationally healthy.

Be open, regardless of your theological stance. Stand with your feet slightly closer than shoulder-width apart, your arms crossed across your chest with your hands around the opposite biceps, your head tilted slightly down and slightly to the left. This is the position my friend Al calls the "stern principal." It says, "I've got my eye on you, waiting for you to make one wrong move, take one wrong step, or say or do one wrong thing." It says, "You're wrong, and I'm right."

It's what, in the customer service world, they call a closed posture. It reinforces that minds are already made up, cases are closed, and decisions are final.

For the LGBTQ teen, it reinforces that you are not open to even discussing the very difficult life choices that they are being forced to make every day. Typically, however, it's not a *physical* posture that communicates this. We communicate it with unthoughtful words and/or disregard for feelings.

I have found that choosing an open posture—physically and otherwise—with LGBTQ youth creates opportunities for ministry where a closed posture would not.

Some of my more conservative ministry friends are probably bristling about now: "You can't be open about what the Bible teaches so clearly.

Homosexuality—and all its associated letters—is wrong. Case closed."

But my decision to be open towards LGBTQ youth is not a theological one. It is, in fact, a practical one. I have come to be comfortable with a fair amount of tension between my theological view on sexuality and my practical response to those whose sexuality doesn't fit within it.

> "...What they really need is not another person to argue with but someone to open their arms and demonstrate love in the most practical sense."

I'm okay with believing that being gay is "wrong" or that marriage should be between one man and one woman or that gender is determined by our chromosomes—and still allowing for a student who doesn't believe those things to feel welcome in my ministry. I'm okay with listening to that person's viewpoint, their story, and their struggle.

Good and godly men and women have disagreed on this topic openly for several decades now—and undoubtedly for much longer in the back halls and student lounges of seminaries around the world. I often find the discussion to be healthy and helpful and those who discuss it to be both passionate and gracious.

But for our youth who have argued it over and over in their minds, on countless sleepless nights, what they really need is not another person to argue with but someone to open their arms and demonstrate love in the most practical sense.

Be about Jesus. When I was a kid, our family had a AAA membership. Sure, there was some value in that if your car broke down, they would send someone to help. But for me, the real value was in the TripTik.

For those of you who grew up in a MapQuest or GPS generation, a TripTik was a custom, multi-page map of the route you'd be taking on your family vacation. Some nice clerk in the AAA office would select pre-printed pages and highlight the route, then bind it into a flip-book of sorts with a spiral-thingy at the top.

I loved to follow along. I'd watch out the window for street signs that told me what highways we were crossing, then frantically flip through the book until I found the spot where we were—eager to circle it and announce to the car that we were "right here." Unfortunately, by the time I'd find the spot on the map, we had already gone way beyond it. "You are here," it seems, only works when you're not moving.

I love Mark 2, especially verse 15, which says that not only did Jesus eat with tax collectors and sinners but there were many tax collectors and sinners who followed him. I think the prevailing view in the evangelical church has been that this simply cannot be when it comes to sexuality: You either give up your life of sin and follow Jesus or you aren't really following Jesus.

But that view assumes a view of salvation that looks a lot like a point on a map, rather than a route on a map. And salvation is often referred to in a present and ongoing way. (Look at 1 Corinthians 1:18 and 2 Corinthians 2:15, for example.[4]) And the idea that we "are being saved" allows for the possibility that we can be followers of Christ, much like the tax collectors and sinners, but not yet have worked out all of our sin issues.

So, can an LGBTQ teen be a Christian? Absolutely. They can be actively following and pursuing Christ and yet not have worked out all of their issues.

---

4. In 1 Corinthians 1:18, we read: "For the word of the cross is foolishness to those who are perishing, but to us who are being saved it is the power of God" (NASB). Then in 2 Corinthians 2:15: "For we are a fragrance of Christ to God among those who are being saved and among those who are perishing" (NASB). Both passages affirm an understanding of salvation consistent with an ongoing, present tense. I'm not a theologian; but, practically speaking, I have found that none of us seem to have arrived at the state God ultimately intends for us. Further, 2 Corinthians 3:18 reminds us that this transformation is ongoing in our lives: "And we all, who with un-veiled faces contemplate the Lord's glory, are being transformed into his image with ever-increasing glory, which comes from the Lord, who is the Spirit".

Much of my ministry career has been in settings with transient populations of students. I spent ten years in ministry on a college campus and now have been two years in ministry at a residential care facility for youth in crisis.

In each of these settings, young people were coming from a variety of church backgrounds; and some had never stepped foot in a church before. In addition, I have always been able to count on having something between six months and two years (on average) with any student. This has forced me to be hyper-intentional about focusing on core doctrines and essential gospel truth. Ultimately, I have been intentional about frequently introducing young people to Jesus, inviting them to follow him, and then trusting him to continue the work (as Philippians 1:6 says) on to completion.

Be unshockable. I think I was in college when I first saw two women walking down the sidewalk holding hands. It was just not something we saw in our small Midwestern town. I'm pretty sure I looked, then looked away, then looked again. I wasn't certain what I was seeing, then I was curious, and then upset… all within a few seconds.

Of course, today this has become commonplace. With the proliferation of gay characters on network television shows and access to the internet, many would say we have become desensitized to what may have seemed shocking less than a generation ago. This is becoming our new normal. And while at least four in ten Americans have a close friend or family member who is in the LGBTQ community, the reality is there are still many students and youth workers in many circles across the US who have had very little to no exposure to LGBTQ students.[5]

---

5. Pew's research on this topic presents a thoughtful and purportedly unbiased assessment. It wasn't long ago that such research was largely dismissed by the church because it was often attributed to organizations associated with the "gay agenda." Read the research for yourself at http://www.pewresearch.org/2007/05/22/fourinten-americans-have-close-friends-or-relatives-who-are-gay/. Of particular note is that the smallest percentages of the population with a friend or family member who is gay are among those sixty-five and older and white evangelicals.

I recently spoke with a youth pastor at a large church in a major city near my home who admitted there were likely LGBTQ youth in his ministry, but he didn't know who they would be.

"I don't even know what I'd say if one of my students told me he was gay," he said—even then, a little bit of shock on his face.

All of us will face the edge of our comfort-zone boundaries in ministry. For me, it has come primarily as I have gotten to know dozens of youth who come from backgrounds of abuse and neglect. The things they have experienced are unimaginable and shocking. When they come to my ministry and we meet for an initial spiritual assessment, I frequently find myself having to hide my discomfort with the reality of their lives. I'm sure it shows through, but most of the students I work with have experienced that many times before. And so have our LGBTQ youth.

Pastors and youth workers, swallowing hard and trying not to let it show, will always be a little shocked when a teen they know and love tells them something difficult to hear. And the reality is, it seems an increasing number of the students we serve in our ministries are struggling with issues of sexual identity and orientation. They are trying to make sense of deeply held beliefs and fleeting thoughts, trying to know who they are and how to identify and whether there is a place for them in the church today.

We can show them shock, or we can show them they are loved and welcome in our churches—welcome to wrestle through difficult issues with the support of a youth leader who may not understand what they're going through but is willing to listen, to learn, and to journey with them towards ultimate Christlikeness.

FINAL THOUGHTS

I was barely twenty, still a senior in college, and my wife was expecting our first child. The pains that had developed in my abdomen, I assumed, were sympathy pains for my pregnant wife. The problem was, after she gave birth, my pain didn't go away.

Over the course of four years or so, they got progressively worse. The pain in my side made it hard for me to do the things a young dad and new youth pastor wanted and needed to do. I couldn't wrestle on the floor with my son, and I couldn't play capture the flag like I used to.

Eventually, it got so bad I was hospitalized for a week; yet the doctors still had no answers as to what was causing the pain. Many of my friends and family prayed for my healing. The elders at my home church anointed me with oil, asking God to take away the pain. But still he didn't.

Over and over I asked myself, "If God did not intend for me to live with this pain, then why won't he take it away?" And finally, the answer came: God cared more about my spiritual healing than my physical healing. He cares more about my heart than my body.

This realization brought me great freedom. I gave up pursuing every medical option and began, instead, to pursue the great Healer.

I'm confident it's time for the church to do the same. It's time to shift our attention from how we can "fix" or change LGBTQ people to how we can help them to pursue the God who loves them, the only source of true healing and transformation.

Eventually the pain in my side faded, though it is never truly gone. Like the thorn in Paul's side, I believe the pain I've experienced is a constant reminder to welcome the hurting and broken with grace and mercy and let God be the Healer.

RESPONSE

BY GEMMA DUNNING

I find Eric's approach and commitment to coming alongside LGBTQ youth heart-warming. His pastoral heart for young people shines throughout his writing and, for this, I thank God.

I found myself highlighting and *amen*-ing out loud to much of what Eric has written but particularly felt a sense of connection to his words on young people's identity being rooted in Christ and not in their sexuality or gender orientation; and I agree with him that our role is to point all young people first and foremost toward Christ. We must not forget that our role is to lift eyes up to the Divine and that in doing so we have a distinctly different role than that of support worker or social worker.

I also fully appreciate Eric's call for all youth ministers to being willing to learn from LGBTQ youth. Much of my own journey into this subject has come from a place of recognizing that a) I have a limited knowledge and that b) others have more experience than I do. His call to arms to be genuine in earnestly seeking to learn from LGBTQ youth themselves, rather than what others say about them or how others portray them, is to be commended. But the reality is that this type of learning can only come from a place of authentic relationship with those who identify as LGBTQ. This is a process that does not have a quick-fix solution to it, nor is it a one-size-fits-all approach but rather is something that will require integrity, humility, sensitivity, compassion, and admitting when you make mistakes or get things wrong.

However, Eric and I probably disagree on the aspect of transformation; and, while he has not written extensively about this here, there are hints of it throughout his writing. I fully appreciate the stage at which many of the young people Eric ministers alongside in his role find themselves, but I have seen countless adults who have had the promises of transformation spoken over them as teens only to discover that thirty years have gone by and transformation hasn't happened. Please read me right, I agree that God *can* transform all things. However, this is not the experience I have witnessed nor is it the experience documented by experienced practitioners in this field such as Wendy Vanderwal–Gritter. (See Vanderwal-Gritter's book, *Generous Spaciousness* [Brazos, 2014].) In fact, most headlines attached to transforming ministries come with an abundance of hurt, pain, and devastation for those on the receiving end of the ministry and also for those who surround them.

In the UK, we're seeing more and more LGBTQ Christian adults now emerging, many of whom have lived with, in a sense, double lives as they attempted to live a "transformed life" in the eyes of the church. Many genuinely believing that they have been healed of their sexuality and many more throwing themselves into serving Christ as if good works will aid the transformation process. For far too many, the later realization that transformation hasn't happened brings many practical implications that cause much damage to themselves and those around them.

Many enter into opposite-sex marriages in good faith, only to divorce later—not just to be able to live as their authentic selves but also to enable their spouses to be loved and wanted in the way they deserve to be, by new partners. They may even have children who then also find themselves innocently caught up in this story and the resulting fallout.

In addition, there's often an increased shame an unfulfilled promise of transformation may bring—*If only I'd been more holy, more faithful, prayed more, worshipped more, etc.* This internal sense of failure, in my experience, often leads to depression, even suicidal tendencies, leaving many older LGBTQ people even further ostracised from families, friends, and churches.

My concern though, for the purpose of discussion here, is more that a theology of transformation *does* profoundly impact the practice of the youth minister and ultimately the relationship between the minister and youth. So, while Eric calls for us to be open to LGBTQ youth regardless of our theological stance, I really struggle to see how we can genuinely minister with a sense of integrity and authenticity if sitting at the root of our theological view is that this is something foundational in an LGBTQ youth that God needs to transform.

It seems like a tension that most of us as youth ministers would not be able to hold well—to love, accept, and encourage someone while all the time internally praying and hoping for a significant shift in who they are. This speaks volumes to the person on the receiving end of our care that we see their nature as ultimately flawed. (And this conflict stands whether we are even speaking of actual same sex *practice* or transgender shift.)

In short, I'm all for the transformational work of God in the lives of teenagers. But let's not make that the focus when it comes to LGBTQ youth and their questions or attraction or identity.

VIEW 4: RADICAL WELCOME

BY SHELLEY DONALDSON

"How do I pastor an LGBTQ youth?"

That's the message I found sitting in my inbox from a fellow youth worker back in the summer of 2016. In fact, I've gotten that question more times than I can count over the past ten years. This time, it was from a beloved friend serving a church deep in Alabama, and I could read the discomfort in his email at even having to ask. He was a socially progressive Christian who worked hard to support LGBTQ people in his community, but tackling the question of ministering to a youth in his congregation who identified as LGBTQ was a much bigger issue than even he imagined. As much as I hate that question, it's a hard and important question we have to answer.

Unfortunately, it's a question that assumes that LGBTQ youth need something special or different than other youth. And, as a youth worker, I believe that all youth should be treated the same. But really, it is a fair question; and I honestly wonder if the people who have asked me that over the years have really wanted to know what I think the answer is. Because I think the answer is hard and messy and involves living into a gospel that we already claim to follow but fall short of every day of our lives.[1]

So, just what does the answer to our question look like? Well, it looks like reconciliation, reparations, hard conversations, open hearts and minds, radical welcome that most of us think we are practicing but really aren't, and most of all grace on all sides of the table.

As youth workers and youth pastors, our job is to advocate for all young people, especially the ones who have been marginalized by the church, and get those people in the pews on board. No, I'm not trying to sell you on a pyramid scheme. I'm trying to say that our youth programs are part of a whole church; and it's not enough just to get our parents, adult volunteers, and non-LGBTQ youth on board with learning how to minister to these particular youth. We have to change the whole church. We minister to those youth by practicing radical welcome in the whole church.

It's worth repeating: *How does one minister to LGBTQ youth?[2] You minister to LGBTQ youth by practicing radical welcome and hospitality as an entire church.* Every community is different and what works for one church won't work for another. But we have to try. We have to change the church before we can effectively minister to LGBTQ youth, so that they know and believe in the love of God and the saving grace and redemption that we have through Jesus Christ. We have to change our church culture, and it starts with conversations and the practices of welcome and hospitality.

So, what happens when you take a church that wants to welcome all

---

1. As a good Presbyterian, much of the theology of my origin is steeped in John Calvin's theology of total depravity. To break (and water) that concept down: No matter what, we all fall short, but our job is to keep on trying and God still loves us and offers us grace even before we can ask for it.

2. I approach this question with the premise that all of God's creation is good and beloved, without conditions. If you believe that God's love comes with the condition that we change and conform to a heteronormative world, then this chapter may not seem relevant for you. But I hope you'll keep an open mind. (For more on *heteronormative*, see the Glossary on page 135.)

people, root itself in the love of God, and really and truly try to live into that love?[3] First, you get people living into the *kin*-dom[4] of God, and that is truly to be celebrated. Second, you get a big mess and hard change.

Let me explain…

MY JOURNEY

Our churches have been set up as places where people are welcome… but not really. We have all heard the age-old saying: The most segregated time of the week is on Sunday mornings in church services. Our churches are made up of people who are like us.

I, for one, was raised to believe that was how it was supposed to be. And until I was in seminary, I believed in that truth. Then I came out of the proverbial closet, and I realized that nothing in me had changed. I was, in fact, the same person as before. I had just learned to embrace myself in a fuller way, and I didn't have to pretend that I was dating men when I talked to my mother.

I remember a distinct conversation with a family member while on a drive before I came out. The Presbyterian Church (USA), the denomination I was raised in, was beginning to really talk about the ordination of gays and lesbians. "I think that gays and lesbians have a place in the church," my relative said with confidence.

"So do I." I responded.

---

3. When I use the term *welcome*, I also assume that the intention of offering hospitality comes with that.

4. I use the term "kin-dom" instead of "kingdom" as a gender-neutral word. "King" refers to a male ruler, where "kin" refers to the idea of family; thus, thinking of God's plan for all humanity as being *together*—God's creation that is one family.

"I think that if gay and lesbian people want to be pastors, then they are best equipped to pastor churches of gay and lesbian people."

"Of course. How else are gay or lesbian youth going to be able to connect with a pastor who is straight?" I eagerly chimed in. I was quite proud of myself at the time for my obviously progressive views.

But I didn't get it on so many levels.

First, LGBTQ people are actually capable and called to minister to all kinds of people. Most of the people in my denomination (PCUSA) identify as cisgendered[5] heterosexuals, but there is no reason why LGBTQ people aren't called into the priesthood of all believers just like anyone else. Second, all LGBTQ people have a place in God's church. The church has just kept us out and called us "other" for so long that we oftentimes think there's not a place for us or that that place is limited.

I was lucky. I came from a small church outside Atlanta that loved me and reminded me that no matter what I was created, loved, called, and claimed by God and had a place in God's great big choir. I was never treated as the "other." This church was a saving grace for me as a twentysomething-year-old, coming out while in seminary. But there are so many others, primarily teenagers, who aren't hearing that message of love and acceptance; and for so many reasons, we have to make sure they hear it and believe it.

And we, the church, have to mean it. Here's where things start to get messy.

---

5. *Cisgendered* refers to someone who identifies with the biological sex they were assigned at birth. For instance: I was born a female, and I identify as one in my adult life. (See p. 135.)

WHAT DRIVES MY VIEW

If you've ever browsed through the Gospels, you know that Jesus' message was radical for his time. And if you didn't know that, news flash: *It's super radical!* Jesus has dinner with tax collectors and other people considered sinners for his time (Mark 2). He called for children to be brought to him instead of turning them away (Matthew 19; Luke 18). Jesus hung out with Samaritans (John 4) and helped lepers (Luke 5); and we all know the story of our favorite wee little man, Zacchaeus: the tax collector everyone loved to hate (Luke 19).

Here's the thing: Jesus' message is radical for our time as well. How often have we put conditions on others before actually welcoming them? And we aren't just talking church but everyday life. We are a world built on the expectation of conformity.[6] We have built our churches as places to conform, not transform.

Now, you might be thinking, "Well, Christianity is about conforming to Jesus' message." Yes. You'd be right. But nowhere does Jesus say, "You have to *not* be a tax-collector, or a prostitute, or Samaritan, or be straight, or whatever to follow my way." Jesus' welcome wasn't and still isn't exclusive. Neither should Jesus' church be.

> "We have built our churches as places to conform, not transform."

Jesus' Message of Welcome

If we want to create spaces and communities that transform hearts, minds, and lives for Jesus and his teachings, then we have to do like he did and welcome everyone into God's house, no matter what. Again, this is where it gets messy. Because if we want to truly welcome others into God's church, we have to be willing to give up our ideas about conformity. We have to be willing to truly accept people where and how they are and help them live into their lives

---

6. Check out Kristin Houghton's article in *The Huffington Post* from 2010, for a good argument of the problems of conformity: http://www.huffingtonpost.com/kristen-houghton/being-different-the-sadne_b_766626.html.

fully, without an agenda on changing who it is God has created them to be. Practicing the "love the sinner, hate the sin" theology won't cut it. Jesus' welcome and love didn't come with conditions, nor should ours.

Truly welcoming people in the name of Christ is hard because it causes us to re-think everything we know about being the church. It calls us to throw away our ideas of how we think *others* should be and examine *ourselves* and our own behaviors. Welcoming in the name of Jesus means changing the way we've been doing things for so long. Welcoming in the name of Jesus means being radical and different and going against the grain of society in a world bound up and built upon conformity.

I'm assuming that if you're reading this, then you're ready or at least willing to consider some changes. Or maybe you're just curious and not sure you agree with all of this. Either way, I'm glad you're here.

What's at Stake
We have all heard the statistics of young people (aka: Millennials and Generation Z) today and their departure from the church. They see the church as hypocritical. The church claims to love and welcome all, but instead they see the church and its leaders condemning the LGBTQ community. They see in the media how the church spends money on the lavish lives of their pastors who turn around and preach a prosperity gospel. They watch as the church picks the side of the wealthy when it comes to politics. They see how the church fails over and over in our broken world to try and bring about healing. What we don't often look towards are the ways in which the church gets it right, or at least is trying to. And we *have to* try. We have to speak up and out against those things that are hypocritical and hurtful, like the ways in which we treat people who are considered *other* to the church.

What's at stake is not only the future of the church, but the lives of the people who have been labeled as *other* by the church in one way, shape, or form. What's at stake is the gospel and living it out in the world. The church has spent so long trying to label everyone else who isn't like them as an *other* that we've lost sight and created a church that condemns and oppresses instead of one that builds up and creates community.

What's at stake is the ingrained trauma that the church has caused LGBTQ people. And as long as the church continues to see LGBTQ people as *other*, then that trauma will continue on

"Practicing the 'love the sinner, hate the sin' theology won't cut it. Jesus' welcome and love didn't come with conditions, nor should ours."

and on. Our job, as God's people who claim to be followers of Jesus Christ, is to reverse the trauma caused by the church, to right the wrong, and to make reparations. We not only need reconciliation but we need to mend the hearts broken—ours and God's.

In his book, *The Wounded Heart of God: The Asian Concept of Han and the Christian Doctrine of Sin*, author Andrew S. Park explores the concept that when we hurt one another (as in, when we sin toward others), we not only wound the other and ourselves in the process, but we also wound God and God's heart.[7] We sin against our neighbor and we sin against God. There are scars left on the person doing the harming, on the heart of the one who is harmed, and upon God because God is present in all that we do and in who we are. We must not only repent and forgive, but we must heal the *han*. *Han* is a Korean word and does not have an equivalent word in English. But it can best be described as grief, sorrow, spite, resentment, etc.

Our job is to heal the *han* of the LGBTQ community. And to do that, we've got some hard and messy work ahead.

Radical Welcome: Spelling It Out

In July of 2017, our head pastor gave a sermon about the state of things in our church. Particularly, how our church is perceived by people outside our own walls. To give you some background, our

---

7. Andrew S. Park, *The Wounded Heart of God: The Asian Concept of Han and the Doctrine of Sin* (Nashville, TN: Abindgon Press, 1993).

church has been a welcoming community for LGBTQ people since before I moved to Chicago in 2009. And it's rare for such a large church in a mainline denomination to take such a stance; but with lots hard work, we have come to the place where we have claimed that part of ourselves. However, while we practice complete and radical welcome inside of our church walls, most people who walk past our gothic building on Chicago's Magnificent Mile on Michigan Avenue would never know that we have open lesbians and gay men on staff and in our pulpits. That is where we were failing and what our pastor brought to light in her sermon. We had to make sure all people knew that everyone was welcome in God's church.

It's really easy to claim to be a welcoming church, and the people within the walls may truly know that and believe it in their hearts. But it doesn't mean a thing without showing it. If you can talk the talk, you better start practicing how to walk the walk. It's like I tell the teenagers in my youth group, "I don't need you to be able to preach the gospel; I need you to be able to practice it, so that others see the gospel in action through you."

I can't count the number of churches in the last year that I have interviewed with for associate and solo pastor positions, all over the United States, who have said something in the realm of "we are fine with gays and lesbians; we are totally supportive." The problem is, there is nothing to indicate that on their website, on their materials, or in talking to them. The only way to find it out is to ask. And who wants to do that? It's already uncomfortable enough to have to come out as a lesbian in a job interview and then ask if that's cool with them. Why not just put it in writing? Why not extend the hospitality and offer that information up front?

And just to be clear, it's not enough to put that a church is "a welcoming community to all God's people" on a church mission or belief statement. No. It literally has to be spelled out. There are plenty of churches that claim to welcome everyone, but how is a person who is LGBTQ supposed to decipher if they really mean it or if they really mean "we welcome people if they are a good fit into what we think they should or shouldn't be"? It's not enough to say that a church welcomes everyone. You've got to spell it out.

Here's the difference. Instead of writing that you are simply a "welcoming" church, tell people exactly *who* you welcome. Don't assume. Never assume. If you assume anything, assume that the people reading your mission or belief statement are people looking for a church community and know nothing about you. Say something like…

> *We welcome all people, regardless of race, sexual identity, gender, etc. And we affirm that all of God's creation, no matter what their background, social status, economic means, or otherwise, is loved and good and has a place in this world and in this church.*

Spell it out. Assume they know nothing. Because when the young person who is looking to hear that God loves them sees that statement (when all they have

"Instead of writing that you are simply a 'welcoming' church, tell people exactly *who* you welcome."

ever heard is how wrong they are and that they need to change), they will know they have a safe space and that there are people of faith who will truly try to welcome them with open arms. The LGBTQ community has been taught, through experience, that welcome does not always mean everyone. That is the first step in ministering to LGBTQ youth. Make sure they know, without an arguable doubt, that they are welcomed into your community with intentional, radical welcome and love.

But for Pete's sake, don't say it unless you absolutely, positively mean it.

For some churches, this will be quick and relatively painless. For others, it will seem like far more than baby steps; it will be as though you're writing a whole new theology. And what do we do when we are nervous or fearful of change? We cling to the old and are hesitant to embrace the new.

Changing Hearts

Intentional conversations must be had by all the church, not just those on committees or boards who make the decisions, but your entire church. Hard ones that might break with old traditions. Conversations about how to welcome people better. It means that we, God's people, have to look inward to find out how we are doing welcome and hospitality wrong when we believe we've done such a good job at it for all these years. Because we have, but we can do better. It means changing. And change is hard.

In their book, *Switch: How to Change Things When Change Is Hard*, brothers Chip and Dan Heath explain change as having two active participants: the elephant and the rider.[8] The elephant is the *heart* of a person. It's the thing that is big and unwieldy and has emotions and will make decisions, big and small, based on those emotions. When we are in panic mode, most of us turn to our hearts and go with that. When I'm stressed or facing huge change, I often give in to my own emotional needs in the form of fried chicken, grits, biscuits, and pimento cheese. I know that I don't need all these high-calorie foods, but I'm an emotional eater. It's how I deal with things when I feel stressed out. Even though I know there are better and healthier ways, my elephant (my emotions, my *heart*) seeks out the things that comfort me and help me to feel safe.

On the other side of the equation is the rider that sits atop the elephant: the *mind* of a person. While it might seem superior, the rider loses to the will of the elephant more times than not. If the elephant wants a cookie, unless it truly chooses to believe that the cookie is bad for it, the elephant will have its cookie. Even when the rider knows that cookies have calories and something healthier should be eaten in its place, unless the elephant truly is changed to believe that as well, then the rider will have to go in the direction of the elephant and have a bite. Even though my rider mind knows that one person should only eat so much pimento cheese on biscuits in one setting, my elephant heart knows no limits.

---

8. Chip Heath and Dan Heath. *Switch: How to Change Things When Change Is Hard* (New York: Crown Publishing, 2010).

Not the best analogy, but you get the point. People go with their emotional elephants. If we want to welcome and minister to LGBTQ young people, we have to change the hearts of people. Minds are easily changed, but the heart—the unwieldy, big and determined elephant—is where it's at. Our hearts are connected to the traditions and regular ebbs and flows of our churches. Our hearts have made it this far, so why change now? Our hearts will feel the pain of people leaving our churches because they don't agree with changes to be more inclusive and welcoming. Our minds can tell us the statistics about LGBTQ youth suicide and the number of youth who are bullied online and in their schools and in social circles for being different, and we can believe those. But until our hearts are changed and can truly feel those numbers in terms of people that are loved by God, then nothing will change. The elephant will continue to do what it has always done.

So, we have to go for the hearts of people. There have to be conversations, real and honest ones, before any of those mission or belief statements can ever change.

> "If we want to welcome and minister to LGBTQ young people, we have to change the hearts of people."

Before we can make sure those young people will recognize our welcome on the church website and the signs outside our front doors, we have to change our hearts. Then our outward appearances will change to reflect the people on the inside of the buildings.

Preparing to Be a Safe Place

Whether or not your entire church gets on board, you've still got a job to do; and if you've got LGBTQ youth, you not only have a job but a big responsibility. As I stated before, there's an ingrained trauma within the lives of LGBTQ people, and it starts young. They see the media and hear the statements that churches make. They feel the microaggressions of others on a daily basis. And, depending on the community they live in, they may feel petrified to come out or even to think about their sexuality for fear of the consequences. This is why the church needs to truly be that safe space for all.

Part of our job as youth workers and pastors is to change that trauma and help heal it. Remember the *han* I mentioned earlier from Park's book? That's what we have to address if we want to minister to LGBTQ youth effectively and realistically. We have a responsibility to reconcile the past of the church and its oppression of people who are "other" and then take it a step further and make some reparations. We have to heal the ingrained trauma that the church has set upon the hearts of these people. If we don't heal the trauma ingrained in these young people, we fail to minister to them as we might a non-LGBTQ youth when they have experienced a traumatic life situation.

Here's the fun part: There's no one way to do this. But here are some great ways to start:

First off, do your homework. Grab your Bible, some commentaries by writers *with different points of view*, and grab a copy of Dr. Daniel A. Helminiak's book, *What the Bible Really Says About Homosexuality*.[9] Then go. Delve into the texts that people have used for centuries to condemn homosexuality. Don't just read the Scripture and determine what you think it means in your head; go talk to scholars and pastors about it. Do your homework! If you believe that ministering to LGBTQ youth is important, then you have to do your homework.

Second, look around you. Check out what other denominations and churches are saying about how they welcome and minister to LGBTQ people. There are some great resources, scholars, and churches that are doing it right.

Third, take a good long look at your church. Be honest about the baggage that your church community has. If your church family has a history of condemning LGBTQ people (which many do at some point), then be honest about it. That's a burden that we must uncover and carry with us. But it's what we do with it that ultimately matters. You can't truly love and minister to LGBTQ people until you've been

---

9. Daniel A. Helminiak, *What the Bible Really Says About Homosexuality* (Tajique, NM: Alamo Square Press, [1994] 2000).

honest about who you have been.

Preparing Your Youth

I think it's normal for most of our church people to assume that young people, our teens, are fine with change. We assume they like to shake up the boat and do things differently. We assume they prefer contemporary worship services over traditional ones. We assume they want pop culture to be part of their faith. We have lots of assumptions about our young people. But we do them a disservice to make those assumptions about any of them, LGBTQ or not.

The community of youth I serve does not, in fact, care for what most would label "contemporary worship." In fact, if a song doesn't come out of an approved PCUSA hymnal, our youth often don't know what to do with it. Many of them have labeled a lot of contemporary Christian music as "Jesus is my boyfriend" music and often don't care for it. We can't make assumptions about any of our youth and what they want or believe, because it spans the spectrum. And we have to honor that.

Recently, I met with some of the youth from a large church in the Southeastern United States. I was asked to come and speak about LGBTQ issues. This church is considered a very large and progressive church in our denomination, much like the church I serve. Most of the youth in that church were welcoming of LGBTQ youth and, in fact, wanted to find ways to be more openly supportive so that other youth knew they were welcome without any stipulations. But a few of the youth were clearly struggling with this on a theological level. They were still holding on to the belief that the only valid relationship was one where one man and one woman were together in a marriage that was blessed by God. This is where they were at. They wanted to be welcoming and be inclusive, but they weren't there yet. And it's our job to help them get there.

We cannot ignore those students who aren't there yet. If we believe in the priesthood of all believers, that all of God's children really do have a place in the choir, then we have to understand that we minister to one another. The youth in our programs minister to one another just as much as we do. So, we have to help them along in having conversations, Bible studies, Sunday morning reflections, and so on. We have to help them see the message of Christ as one that fully embraces each and every person just where they are.

If you want to minister to LGBTQ youth in positive and healthy ways, you have to have those hard conversations with your youth. Two documentaries I always recommend watching with your youth are *Fish Out of Water*[10] and *For the Bible Tells Me So.*[11] *Fish Out of Water* examines the texts that have been traditionally used to condemn LGBTQ people by speaking with biblical scholars and LGBTQ people who have lived through being harassed and condemned with these texts. In *For the Bible Tells Me So*, the filmmakers interview different families going through the typical struggles of families of faith who have a loved one who identifies as LGBTQ and the challenges of their churches. Both are emotional, and I suggest watching them *before* showing them to your youth. That way, you are ready to answer questions and lead discussions. You can even go to the resources pages on their respective websites for study guides and discussion starters.

Watching these films and talking about them together is by no means the end of the conversation with your youth, but it's a good starting place.

Accepting That What We Say Matters

Language. It's what has defined us for centuries. We spend hours and hours of our lives learning languages, practicing them, deciphering them, trying to master them. Language matters. It matters when someone gets your name wrong. Especially when you've told them a thousand times.

There was a pastor I worked with several years ago when I was a camp

---

10. Ky Dickens, dir. *Fish Out of Water* (documentary), Yellow Wing Productions, 2009: fishoutofwaterfilm.com.

11. Daniel Karslake, dir. *For the Bible Tells Me So* (documentary), Atticus Group, 2007: forthebibletellsmeso.org.

director; and over the course of a year, this pastor and I had multiple interactions with one another. But even after reading my name on paper and seeing me with my nametag on—despite all the times I corrected her and told her my actual name, never once did she ever get my name right. *Shelby* is not the same as *Shelley*. Sure, it sounds similar, but it's not the same. No matter what, this pastor would introduce me as Shelby, call me Shelby, and address all emails to me as Shelby.

This pastor was a perfectly nice woman. She was good at her job and really cared about her people and her ministry work. But she never got my name right. While it may sound as though I'm being petty, it hurt my feelings on multiple occasions because that's not my name. For someone to be corrected on multiple occasions and still not even attempt to correct themselves was insulting and disrespectful. What it said to me was that she wasn't willing to try and see me for who I was, all because of her inability to learn my name.

Names are identity markers for us. They are important; and we spend a lot of time explaining them, living into them, making sure that when people hear our names, they associate them with positive attributes about us. I was named after my mother's childhood best friend from Sunday school. That is a part of my name and my story. It's part of who I am. It helps to identify me as a female, and identifying as a female is important to me. I want to be recognized as a female when I am out in public. Not because I need the whole world to know I'm a woman, but because it's part of who I am.

On the same note, LGBTQ people need to be seen for who they are; and sometimes this comes in the form of a name change or pronoun usage. We don't all identify with the sex we were identified with at birth. Or maybe we do, but we don't live into our gender in the ways that society has set out for us.

One simple practice is to ask pronouns.[12] Simply ask: "What are

---

12. **Editor's Note:** For more on this, see Audrua Welch Malvaez's specific advice about asking for pronouns on p. 127.

the pronouns that you identify with?" I know; it sounds odd and different. But it's important. What harm does it do to those youth who identify with the pronouns that we perceive them to have? None.

On the other hand, what does it do for that one youth who identifies with pronouns that aren't what people might perceive? It tells them, "We want to know, honor, and respect you for who you are." And what that does is widen the circle a little more.

Recently, I was leading a training for a large group of youth leaders at a conference. Almost all of these thirty-eight leaders were seasoned youth workers and pastors. When I asked people to go around and introduce themselves to the group, I also asked them—if they felt comfortable with it—to give us the pronouns they identified with. "I'll go first," I said. "My name is Shelley. I am from Chicago, and the pronouns I identify with are female pronouns like *she* and *her.*"

Not all the leaders felt comfortable giving their pronouns, and that was fine. They weren't forced to. But by practicing something as small as asking people the pronouns they should be addressed by, you let that one youth in your group know that they are welcomed and loved; and you honor the reality that they might not fit into the mold the church so often creates for gender and sexuality.

Now, let me be clear, this isn't just something to do in a large group. Asking an individual what they would like to be called is important as well. Remember that rider and elephant from earlier? This is one of those things that triggers a lot of elephants. Because it's a change from the normal way we do things. Most people are not used to asking someone what pronouns they should use. It takes time, practice, and maybe even some education. (A great tool for learning about pronouns—because it can be exhausting and is ever-changing—is from the *Minus 18* website.)[13]

Following up on these conversations by actually using the pronouns

---

13. This short video and interactive website gives examples of how to use pronouns that are different or gender-neutral in everyday vernacular: https://minus18.org.au/index.php/resource-packs/pronouns.

and/or names is even more important. It can feel strange and uncomfortable to use different or gender-neutral pronouns if you've never done so, but it matters.

And be forewarned that the elephant can get even more uncomfortable when you forget or mess up. But it's okay. Apologize, try again, and move on. You won't get it right the first, second, third, fourth, or maybe even the fifth time. But practicing and trying—and helping your other youth practice and keep trying—really matters to that one individual.

Think of it this way. In Luke 15, Jesus tells the parable of the one lost sheep out of one hundred. The shepherd seeks out that one sheep because it is just as important as the other ninety-nine. We have to practice ways to seek out and invite that one sheep back into the fold; and for some, this can be a way to do just that. It's a way to go above and beyond the basic name games and introductions. It is a way of making reparations for the past wounds the church has inflicted in other LGBTQ individuals by saying to the person in front of us, "Who you are matters to us and we will do our best to honor that." It is going a little further for that one sheep to help heal the *han* and change the church.

GETTING PRACTICAL

Now that we've gone over some of the big hard things that have to be tackled to truly minister to LGBTQ people, let's talk about a couple of the practical things you can do to become a truly welcoming church.

Designate a gender-neutral bathroom. I don't know about your church, but the one I grew up in had signs that simply read "washroom." Many churches and other public buildings have signs designating which bathroom you can or can't use, and we all know about the battles in our country over what many are calling "bathroom bills." For someone who does not identify with the gender they were determined to be at birth, this can be frustrating. Even to the point of not attending the church as a result.

This might not seem like ministry, but it is. It's a way to provide hospitality and welcome. I once heard author and speaker Rodger Nishioka tell a room of pastors, "I know how hospitable a church is when I walk in by whether or not I see a sign letting me know where the bathroom is within the first fifteen minutes or if someone offers that information without me having to ask." And he's right.

If you don't already have a family bathroom or a designated gender-neutral bathroom, it's time to make one! There are some churches that have large, multi-stall bathrooms; and that can be tricky. But just find one.

Here's the other catch, however: It shouldn't be the bathroom that's the farthest away. Don't inconvenience or ostracize your LGBTQ youth any more than they already are in life. Let them have a closer bathroom. Ask your cisgendered boys or girls if they mind going to a farther bathroom. Get creative. Have conversations. But *please* do all you can to make them feel included, welcome, and loved. Sometimes hospitality takes the form of a bathroom that *isn't* on the other side of the building.

Be thoughtful about lock-ins. These are some of the foundational memories that so many youth have of their time in their churches. As a youth worker I have a love/hate relationship with them. For our youth, they are a prime chance to have some unstructured time together to play, laugh, share snacks, watch movies, tell horrible jokes, worship, and just spend fellowship time together with very little to no sleep. The two lock-ins I do each year for our senior high youth are two of the most invaluable events that we have, and I wouldn't give them up for anything. (Although, I would give just about anything for a good night's sleep, but such is the life of those dedicated to shepherding God's young people.)

However, lock-ins also present problems. Particularly when it comes to sleeping arrangements (and don't neglect bathrooms at these events either). I am lucky enough to be in a church that is large enough that all youth sleep in one room. We turn on a movie, and—rather than any forced binary gender division—the youth disperse throughout the room, leaving a designated space between each of them so everyone has their own personal space and is comfortable, with adult volunteers dispersing themselves throughout the room. There's plenty of room, and we've never had a problem. But this is not the case for most churches. Maybe you have a small youth room: Go to your fellowship hall, to the sanctuary, or whichever part of your building is large enough for everyone to fit. Maybe your church is too small for that to make sense for your group: Take the lock-in to someone's house and use the living room. Maybe you are in a building with multiple rooms to use: Great! You can still split up the youth, but do it in a way that makes your LGBTQ youth comfortable.

Plan camps and retreats with care. "What should I do about camp?" is another frequently-asked question I get from youth workers when it comes to ministering to

> "Sometimes hospitality takes the form of a bathroom that *isn't* on the other side of the building."

LGBTQ youth. And I never have the perfect answer. Each church is different and some camp situations are easier to adjust than others. It's up to you to get creative, flexible, and inclusive. Some churches and/or camps require that the youth be split into different rooms based on gender. If that's the case, you need to reexamine your church requirements or where you are taking your youth to camp. Maybe you should do a campout with tents instead of going to that big facility you've always used before. Whatever the case, you have a responsibility to offer hospitality to that LGBTQ youth in the name of Christ. If you've got a solution that works in those situations, by all means, tell others about it.

From my days as a camp director, this issue came up at least once a summer. Most church camps saw their heyday in the 1950s or 60s. They probably have brightly colored signs outside the bathrooms that are ancient and just keep getting painted over each summer with a fresh coat that reads "boys" and "girls." Just like in churches, however, it is easy to designate a gender-neutral bathroom there—just stick a "gender-neutral bathroom" sign over it. And if you're taking your youth to a camp that doesn't have one (because, let's be honest, most don't), then don't be afraid to ask for it, even if it's just for your week or weekend of camp. It is your job to advocate for God's children. Same with sleeping quarters. And if you are tent-camping, get one giant tent for everyone.

Explore the Bible *purposefully* with your youth—all of it. This is where that homework from earlier comes in. If you're like so many other youth workers, you only get a few hours per week, maybe even just one, to impart an entire week's worth of spiritual formation to your youth. Our youth today are overcommitted and over-programmed. They are being raised in the fast-paced and competitive world that we have created for them. So, when they come through those doors of the church, it's go time.

Make good use of Sunday mornings and Bible studies. These times together are invaluable. And *this* is where you start to have those conversations.

In your studies with your youth, take the time to delve into the Scriptures with intentionality. Look at the stories used to condemn LGBTQ people. Take for instance Sodom and Gomorrah. This is where we get the term "sodomy" from. We all know the story we were taught: "The men wanted to be with Lot's visitors in a sexual way which was wrong; so God destroyed them." *Wrong.* Read it closely. Look at the text and its history. And see how the Bible itself interprets the story. (See Ezekiel 16:49-50.) Sodom and Gomorrah is about inhospitality; it is about treating others who are different as though they are worthy of gang-rape by the people of Lot's community—all for simply being from outside of their walls. Lot is spared because of his *hospitality.*

We have to re-read the Scriptures with new and curious eyes; we have to be open to different interpretations; and we must encourage this with our youth. We have to be willing to see the Bible as something that is living and breathing and new and fresh each time we look at it. And we have to equip our volunteers and parents to do the same. When we do this, we open up the possibility for an LGBTQ youth to see the Bible as words that speak to them as well. We have to undo the damage done by so many years of harmful biblical scholarship. We have to repair that part of the *han*.

Speaking of which...

Speak carefully about God. Remember how language is important? Well, how you talk about God to your youth is important. Our default is to use male pronouns for God. This is fine. But how inclusive is it? Don't we also hear about God being referred to as a mother figure? (See Isaiah 66:13; Psalm 131:2; and Matthew 23:37.)

If we want to be truly inclusive, we can't gender God. Humans were made in God's image, but what does God's image look like? God came before humans and language and our thoughts.

> "Don't be afraid to be uncomfortable. Don't be afraid of letting your youth, parents, adult volunteers, or church members feel uncomfortable."

So, why do we gender God? God came before our gendered language and our ideas of gender and sexuality. Practice using gender-neutral terms for God.[14]

For many LGBTQ youth, God has been for people who fit into a gender binary.[15] God fits no one's binary because God is bigger than that. And making sure all of your youth know that is important and necessary. This is one way to help your LGBTQ youth know that God is bigger than just heterosexual males and females and that God is connected to each and every one of us.

---

14. Let's be clear: I am not saying that we should stop using male pronouns for Jesus. Jesus was a man. We have historical evidence of that.

15. This is when we put people's sex and gender into two distinct forms of masculine and feminine. (See the Glossary on p. 135.)

FINAL THOUGHTS

Don't be afraid to be uncomfortable. Don't be afraid of letting your youth, parents, adult volunteers, or church members feel uncomfortable. LGBTQ people have felt uncomfortable their entire lives; it won't hurt the majority to feel the discomfort of the minority. That's called empathy. We should all have it in great abundance. Without it, we can never repair the *han* of LGBTQ people.

Sit in the discomfort of knowing that we can be better. Sit in the discomfort of knowing that we will make mistakes. Sit in the discomfort that comes with doing something different and trying to change. Sit with your elephant when it becomes stressed or afraid. Being willing to sit in that discomfort means a lot to those who have been uncomfortable in a heteronormative world. It means you're searching for that welcome and hospitality. *This is how we start to make reparations and live into reconciliation.*

Nothing about the gospel is easy. Nothing about Jesus' message is comfortable. What is comfortable is to simply live within our own complacent, cozy lives we have created for ourselves and never be inconvenienced. It is more comfortable to pass someone who is different than engage them.

One thing I have learned from my work with people who have experienced homelessness in their lives is that sometimes the most important thing you can do is to look someone in the eyes—to intentionally see them, to connect with them even if just for a moment. Do that. Find ways to look your LGBTQ youth in the eyes and see them for all God made them to be. See them for who they are.

See them as God sees them.

RESPONSE

BY NICK ELIO

I really appreciate Shelley's perspective; and Shelley and I agree on many things, which I'm glad to discover. It's good to read that there are other youth workers out there fighting the good fight, making the same priorities, and taking similar steps to welcome LGBTQ teenagers into the church.

And I agree with Shelley when it comes to what is at stake. Statistics tell us there are over 5,000 teenage suicide attempts a day. That's a lot of lives at stake. And I also appreciate Shelley pointing out that *the future of the church* is at stake. I don't think that either of us is suggesting or believes that this one issue could take down God's church, but our response moving forward will contribute to what sort of influence the church may have down the road. The fact of the matter is people are leaving. People are pointing out inconsistencies and hypocrisies, and they won't continue to participate in the way that generations before them did if these issues are not addressed. Many of my fellow Millennials (and others) believe that if the Good News isn't for everyone, then it isn't for anyone; and how we continue to respond as the church to our LGBTQ friends matters.

I also wholeheartedly agree with Shelley's insistence that churches must spell out their stance on the matter. If your church is welcoming and/or affirming of the LGBTQ community, let people know. If it's not, be clear about that as well. Just recently I spoke with a man at our church who told me that he was gay. It was his first Sunday with us and he had been hurt badly by the church he had been at previously. That church had advertised itself as a safe place for all people, that they had a "come as you are" mentality and that "all are welcome." But as soon as he began to take further steps towards community and volunteering, he found out that wasn't at all the case. Turns out there was a glass ceiling for LGBTQ people and their level of involvement in that community. And once he asked more directly, he was told that when it came homosexuality they were a "Bible-believing church," as if to imply that anyone who felt differently doesn't believe in the Bible.

As he told me this story, he pantomimed a knife being stabbed through his heart as he explained the hurt this church had caused him. So, when he googled "LGBTQ friendly churches," found our church website, and found all the information about our position, he did not need to enter our building with any fear or anxiety. He knew exactly where we stood. (By the way, there is a great resource called ChurchClarity.com that has created a growing database to discover where specific churches fall in the LGBTQ conversation.)

That said, one place where it feels like Shelley and I may disagree would be her section on "Changing Hearts." I get and understand Shelley's desire to help people change their views on LGBTQ people. I often feel that myself, especially when their views are rooted in hate or ignorance. Wanting to educate people and help move them towards greater love and acceptance is important.

But I'm sensing a bit that Shelley would like everyone to be at a place where they can affirm LGBTQ people and relationships. And while it would be nice for us all to be able to agree, I don't see that is a prerequisite for community or belonging. We will never all agree on whether or not we can affirm LGBTQ relationships. Just as the church doesn't agree on our theology of heaven and hell, or Eucharist, or the meaning of all the parables. But there is space and grace for us to be in different places, to be on our own journeys; and the lack of agreement in this conversation does not need to be a deal breaker.

I believe firmly that unity is more important than uniformity; and admittedly, this is where things gets messy. Unity takes those in the Christian LGBTQ community and Christians who affirm them being willing to journey with folks who may not affirm. And it also requires Christians who won't affirm LGBTQ people to journey in faith, without prejudice, alongside those they may disagree with on this point, including LGBTQ Christians themselves. This is what dynamic and diverse community looks like, rooted in the heart of Jesus.

In her chapter, Shelley says, "Truly welcoming people in the name of Christ is hard because it causes us to re-think everything we know about being the church. It calls us to throw away our ideas of how we think *others* should be and examine ourselves and our own behaviors." I couldn't have said it better. So figuring out how to be welcoming to LGBTQ people while still being welcoming to those who can't affirm LGBTQ people has to be a piece of that puzzle.

A NOTE ABOUT THE APPENDICES

When we framed out the concept of this book, I (Marko) was regularly being asked two questions (or variations of them) by youth workers:

1. "I recently had one of my youth group kids come out to me. What should I do?"
2. "I have a transgender teenager who wants to come to summer camp, and I have no idea what to do. Help!"

Actually, since we started working on this book, I'm being asked some form of these two questions with more and more regularity.

We made a choice fairly early on that we wanted our four main writers to focus on the LGB part of LGBTQ. The reason for this is that while the anxiety *you* might experience as a youth worker trying to lovingly respond to teenagers wrestling with *attraction* issues is similar to the anxiety you may experience when teenagers are wrestling with gender *identity* issues, the issues themselves are actually quite different.

While issues of bullying, acceptance, increased suicide rates, and increased rates of depression are critical for both groupings of teenagers (the LBG teens and the TQ teens, if you will), it can easily become diminishing to either set of questions when lumping them all together.

Honestly, dealing with the pragmatic ministry implications of transgender teenagers in your church is, I believe, significantly more complex than the pragmatic ministry implications of gay teenagers in your church. And while we thought it best to focus the bulk of this book on helping gay and SSA teens, we felt we needed to offer you *at least some* thinking on responding to trans teens.

So, we have two appendices for you. In the same spirit as the book, they are intended to get you moving with some direction—providing you fodder for conversations and, possibly, the development of some *practices* or *commitments* (rather than the development of policies).

I wrote the first appendix. It's really an outline more than prose.

Our second appendix came about in the way many of the best collaborations do. Audrua Welch Malvaez, an in-the-trenches youth worker in Texas, emailed me after first hearing we were developing this book and asked if we'd be addressing trans teens. When I explained that we were going to keep our focus primarily on SSA issues, she asked if she could write a chapter or appendix or *something* about responding to transgender students. So, though presented without others "views," we thought her stand-alone piece would be really helpful to you.

APPENDIX 1:
THOUGHTS FROM THE PARENT OF A TRANSGENDER TEEN
by Mark Oestreicher

A friend of mine is the youth pastor at a large conservative evangelical church, and *the camp question* had come up. Specifically, his question to me was along these lines:

> We have a female to male transgender eighth grader. He... she... [**Marko's note:** pronouns are really tough when you first start into these discussions] ...*has been attending our church for a while and has been in a girls' small group. He transitioned to male this school year, using a male name and pronouns; but he's still a part of his previous girls' small group, where he's supported and has important friendships. Summer camp is coming up, and this student is requesting to be in a boys' cabin. His parents, who don't go to our church, have made it clear that this is what they want also.*
>
> *I brought this issue up with our church leadership team; and it very quickly became clear that most of the people on that team had just about zero ability to have a meaningful conversation about it, as they didn't understand even the basics of what transgender means.*
>
> *I paused the conversation and told them I have a friend who has spent more time thinking about this since one of his own children is transgender. How about I have him pull together a bulleted list of talking points for us...?*

That request precipitated a draft of what follows.

■ ■ ■ ■ ■

NOTE: *I am hardly an expert on this topic. I'm mostly just a dad who has walked a journey with my own twenty-three-year-old child; and I'm a youth ministry trainer who seems to find myself regularly wrestling with these questions from other youth workers.*

A few things to understand first:

- LGB and T are not the same issue. L (Lesbian), G (Gay), and B (Bisexual) are about *sexual orientation* (in other words, who is the person *attracted* to). T (Transgender) is about *gender identity* (in other words, what gender do they understand themselves to be).

- The term "transgender" (often shorthanded to "trans") encompasses dozens of subcategories and terms; and those in the transgender community tend to be very intentional about which terms they use for themselves. (For example: My twenty-three-year-old, born female, identifies as *gender neutral* or *gender queer*, meaning that "they"—a plural pronoun—is my child's preference, since English doesn't have a gender-neutral pronoun and my child identifies as both male and female. This is merely one variation of identities under the transgender umbrella, which would include those who are MTF [male to female] or FTM [female to male].)

- The *vast majority* of transgender people would not consider this a "choice" they have made, and would be alienated by language that presumes choosing. Most would say that they have always known, since childhood, that their physical body didn't align with the gender they felt themselves to be.

- The popular concept of a guy who "chooses" to dress as female to gain access to private women's places (bathrooms, changing rooms) is almost entirely urban myth; and the use of opposite-gendered clothing as a "turn on" (called transvestic fetishism) is extremely rare and not at all what being transgender means or even implies.

- Teenagers wrestling with *sexual orientation* issues (LGB) are significantly more likely to be "at risk," particularly when it comes to bullying, depression, and suicide. But teenagers wrestling with *gender identity* issues (T) are exponentially more susceptible to these risks. Most transgender teens believe there are no adults they could turn to for help.

- Non-transgender teenagers (the term for non-trans people, by the way, is cisgendered) have significantly less discomfort with these issues than any older generation. We need to be careful not to project our discomfort onto the majority teenagers in our group.

Some ministry convictions to consider:

- Our preeminent calling is to love. *Love does not require agreement.* And while one might effectively suggest that love and truth are inseparable, one would be hard-pressed to biblically support a commitment to truth *over* love. If anything trumps the other, the sometimes-challenging message of Jesus is to love. Love has no room for disgust. Love chooses to listen. Love does not require change as a prerequisite for genuine relationship.

- In the life of Jesus, we never see theology trumping ministry. Just the opposite is true. I'm not suggesting that theology isn't important (far from it!); but I am suggesting that our first question should always be driven by our role as shepherds rather than our role as theologians or teachers.

- Transgender people are regularly the apex outcasts of our day, particularly in churches. (While you might feel that the cultural tide has turned to being very pro-transgender these days, the everyday experience of transpeople is far from that.) Jesus calls us to the outcasts.

- We *must not* commit the error of assuming we know everything about this issue. We must, of course, make very difficult decisions; but we have to be ruthlessly committed to listening and learning.

Things I needed, as a parent, from my church's youth ministry (that I mostly did not receive):

NOTE: *I am part of a wonderful and thriving church and my two children were very active in the youth ministry. My oldest—my gender queer young adult—participated in just about every way possible* *through high school graduation. I love my church, but the high school ministry at least somewhat dropped the ball when it came to my kid.*

- Of course, *I do not want or need judgment* (on me or on my child). This might sound easier than it is: So many comments and reactions come off as judgment. "*What do you think went wrong?*" or "*What caused this?*" aren't helpful.

- Maybe even more so, *I want compassion but not pity.* Pity comes off as a form of judgment. I find myself instantly distancing myself from people who express pity (or reveal it in their face and body language).
  - Please do ask how I'm doing.
  - Please acknowledge that parenting can be tough.
  - Please ask how you can help.
  - But, personally, I really struggle when people say, "*I'm so sorry for you,*" or simply "*hmmm*" with sad faces, because it sounds like an inference that my kid doesn't meet your approval.
  - Maybe I need the same thing my child needs: *to know that you still want my kid here, even if they don't fit your idea of the ideal youth ministry kid.*

- *I want you to celebrate all that is good and beautiful and true about my child and my relationship with my child.* I need you to NAME those things that are good and beautiful and true. I do *not* need you to quote Bible verses to me.

- *I need you to be a beacon of trust and hope.* It's essential that I know you are trustworthy, or I will never share anything with you again. It's essential that you trust my intentions with my child, whether you agree with me or not. It's essential that you hold hope with and for me: NOT hope that my child will be "fixed" but hope in the reality that God is still at work and has never stopped loving my child or me.

- Finally, to the best of your ability, *I need you to get uncomfortable and go overboard in communicating "We love you and want you here" to my kid.* Without qualifications.

Ministry implications:

- The (genuinely) good intentions of my church's high school pastor and the message received by my kid did not align. He did not intend to be judgmental. But somehow my child perceived that he was communicating a "we love you, but you need to know where we stand" message, which was emphatically received as "you don't belong here" and "I reject you." Our intentions are very important, of course; but our practice must go overboard to stay in alignment with our intentions. And we need to be asking what message is being received. We're the shepherds, and the responsibility resides with us.

- Every case of a transgender teen is unique. And while any youth ministry should have some "practices" in place, each story needs to be heard and considered individually.

- I agree with the teaching North Point Church uses with their youth ministry volunteers: *The church should be the safest place in the world to talk about anything, including same sex attraction* (and, I would add: gender identity).

- Certainly there are people who would disagree with me on this, but I am convinced there is no good reason to *not* use the pronoun a teenager asks you to use. If you need to, just think of it as a nickname. Using any other pronoun *always* communicates (whether we mean to or not) some level of rejection.

- A significant question is the issue of "passing." In other words, if the teen is effectively *passing* (being viewed by others) as their adopted gender, I'd roll with it. If your hope is that they will change, remember…
    - It's not within our power to change anyone (that's the Holy Spirit's work).

○ Gender identity questions, like *all other questions*, are *at the most* secondary to our goal of hearts turned to Jesus.

- Things get a little dicey when it comes to single-gender small group placement. While every case is (as stated previously) unique, and a panacea rule will likely not be helpful in every case, the previous point about "passing" should be considered. If the teenager is viewed as their preferred gender ("preferred gender" might be helpful here, but realize that it can cause offense, just as "birth gender" can) in other contexts (school, home, friends), it likely makes sense to allow for the same at church. But with teenagers, they're often "trying things on" as part of figuring out identity; and if church feels like a safe place, they might want to "try on" being in a differently-gendered small group, while still living into their birth gender in other contexts. In this case, I would lean toward regular conversations (and communication of how much you love them and want them there) coupled with keeping them in the Life Group that gender-aligns with how they're living the bulk of their lives.

NOTE: I wrote "birth gender" in that previous paragraph as to not slow you down on the point I was communicating; but the transgender community strongly prefers "gender assigned at birth" to "birth gender," for reasons I hope are obvious.

- Things *really get complicated* when it comes to youth group trips (anything involving overnight sleeping accommodations or clothes-changing). First, we have to simply admit to ourselves that this is complicated, and it's okay that it's complicated. Admitting to a transgender teen and/or their parents that this is complicated is *helpful* and not a signal of weakness (every day is complicated for them). I suggest a general practice of three options, always informed by conversation and discernment:
  ○ *Accommodation* (allowing the transgender teen to be housed with their preferred gender). I would suggest using this when three realities are in play:
    - The teen is living (and passing) as their preferred gender

in all contexts. (I've known multiple trans teenagers where just about no one knows the "truth" about them.)

- The parents are supportive of this choice.

- The ministry leaders use wisdom and discretion in deciding who should be "in the know" about this, *never* "outing" a teen without their permission.

○ *Neutral space* (creating another option for sleeping space). The upside of this approach is that it honors the student's story and desires, but doesn't put you at risk of dealing with other angry parents or awkward moments in the sleeping space with leaders and other teens. The downside of this is that it *can* be alienating. In many youth ministry contexts, however, this is a best-case scenario. This would still likely need:

- Parents in agreement.

- Another teenager or two (of either gender, though it would be easier for you if the friend was the gender of the trans teen's birth gender) happy to be in that room (a friend) whose parents are also supportive.

- A supportive leader with the same gender as the transgender teen's birth gender.

NOTE: *This would be an option for small group also, to have one gender-neutral small group that a handful of teens could opt into.*

○ *Housed with "birth gender."* I don't believe this should be the default or assumed solution. But there are many instances when it would still be the best choice, even if the transgender teen would prefer otherwise. When this needs to occur, it needs to be accompanied by massive communication of love and acceptance (remember: acceptance of the *person* doesn't have to imply acceptance of every choice they make), follow-up, regular check-ins, and conversations about things *other than* gender identity (no one wants to be known by only this one issue).

REMEMBER: Teenagers are wet cement. Which of us would want to be either alienated because of who we were as teenagers, or still the same person we were then?

APPENDIX 2:
THOUGHTS ON PASTORING TRANSGENDER YOUTH

By Audrua Welch Malvaez

I started my first youth ministry internship when I was eighteen years old, and my first full time and solo gig came along two weeks after I turned twenty-one. There's something unique about being a young twentysomething in youth ministry. All the emotional chaos of adolescence is right in your face when you're pastoring teens, but all the while you are continuously working through your own, more intricate emotional chaos. It creates quite the theological jungle gym. I was learning and experiencing new things that challenged my faith and my understanding of the way God works in the world.

During my summer internships, my mentor Katie had given me a philosophy of youth ministry to use as I developed my ministry practices. It has evolved and shifted as I've gained experience, attended conferences, and networked with other youth workers, but one pillar has always remained the same: My youth ministry will always work to be a place where all who participate feel safe, physically and emotionally.

It's not an unknown to youth workers that being a teen is hard. Our students are constantly under scrutiny for whatever makes them different—whether it's their looks, their income level, their fashion sense, or their hobbies. I've had both "the popular kid" and "the shadow kid" in my office sharing the same story about how they feel left out and too out of place to participate.

We as youth workers have chosen to participate in the lives of our students through the ministry of the church because we believe that Jesus' Word is meant for these young people. Jesus led a life that welcomed all people into his covenant, into his grace. The gospel message of the Scriptures is the truth that God loves us, deeply and passionately, and that we are never alone. We have the honor and privilege of reminding our youth that they are not a mistake and that there is nothing they can do to separate themselves from the love of their Creator.

The Reality of Being Transgender

All of our youth face great difficulties during adolescence. They are trying on different hats, attempting to discover who they are and why they are here. While we walk through life with those who are experimenting in a socially normative way, there are our other teens who are processing or have already processed their gender identities, some of whom we may never know about until years later.

The reality a transgender teenager lives in isn't easy. Being trans, experiences of aggression are more numerous than the norm for many cisgendered persons (individuals who identify as the gender assigned at birth). According to the 2015 US Transgender Survey (USTS):

> "The majority of respondents who were out or perceived as transgender while in school (K-12) experienced some form of mistreatment, including being verbally harassed (54%), physically attacked (24%), and sexually assaulted (13%) because they were transgender. Further, 17% experienced such severe mistreatment that they left a school as a result."[1]

The USTS also studied the faith community of transgender adults and found that "19% of respondents who had ever been part of a spiritual or religious community left due to rejection; 42% of those who left later found a welcoming spiritual or religious community."

As Christians, we are called to love God and love others, accepting God's creations. This is why creating an emotionally safe environment in my ministry is so important to me. I never know what my youth are dealing with when they first walk into my doors; but I want them to leave knowing that they are loved and that they are safe here, no matter what they may be experiencing elsewhere.

---

1. James, S. E., Herman, J. L., Rankin, S., Keisling, M., Mottet, L., & Anafi, M. (2016). The Report of the 2015 US Transgender Survey. Washington, DC: National Center for Transgender Equality, http://www.ustranssurvey.org.

Six months after I started at a church, one of my students, who I'll call Mary, slipped a letter in my hand at the end of youth group. In it, she thanked me for saying on more than one occasion that God loves everybody, even her. Specifically, my use of gender-neutral language for God and using non-gendered terms like "partner" or "significant other" when talking about dating relationships drew Mary out of her head and allowed her to engage with God again.

She told me her story about how she realized she was bisexual and about her discomfort in participating at church because she thought that coming out would mean she'd be kicked out of her leadership positions. This was a mainline Protestant church that had never spoken one way or another about LGBT people, but she still felt as if her church would be ashamed of who she was. At the end of Mary's letter, she thanked me for allowing her space to be comfortable with who she was and expressed hope that others in our youth group would feel the same way she did.

Creating a Safe Space

The question I encounter most frequently from other youth workers who are attempting to navigate ministry with a transgender student is how to work overnight trips. Youth ministry in general has several safe guards in place to protect our students from harm, and we are the unique ministry area that travels with our teenagers without their parents or guardians. In addition to our main goal of providing an opportunity to encounter the presence of the Holy Spirit unencumbered by concerns about their safety, there are a few simple things we can do to keep our transgender youth as emotionally and physically safe as our cisgender youth.

1. Safeguard and provide privacy. All our youth need privacy, but our transgender teens need a different degree of privacy than their peers. Whenever possible, single-use bathrooms are important, even if they aren't in the main facilities but are still accessible, especially when bathing.

2. Make room for choice and agency. Whenever possible, consult transgender students on where they would like to room, what they would like to wear, and what name they would like to go by. If they have friends they are already comfortable with, let them choose who they would like to room with rather than assuming where they would be most comfortable. Better yet, allow everyone to have these options so it's a group norm, not just a special treatment for a certain teenager.

3. Normalize. The most important thing we can do is normalize! It's important for all our youth to not feel odd or out of place, and making this possible for our transgender students only requires awareness and thought on our end. Using non-gendered language like "siblings" or "friends" as opposed to "brothers and sisters," or allowing teens to choose their own color of nametag instead of assigning pink and blue, then drawing attention to common ground activities like who likes dogs or cats, who plays an instrument, etc., are all subtle ways to send a message that we are all unique and we are all able to relate with one another. Combining these kinds of messages with intentional work around individual personhood as part of God's humanity, discussing the *Imago Dei*, allows for safe theological discussion about humankind.

4. Affirm personhood. Get to know what triggers defensiveness in your youth so that you can avoid putting that barrier up between them and God. For example, avoid using the term "preferred" when discussing or asking someone about their pronouns or name. Simply ask, "What are your pronouns?" We all have pronouns and names that we use because they fit us and are appropriate. "People of trans experience" are really just people having experiences in a world with others. They have experiences colored by being transgender just as I have experiences colored by being five feet tall. The most important thing we can do to make our churches safe for all people is to affirm what a person claims as their gender.

Using Your Voice
Our young people are trusting us with their personhood and view us as people who speak with God's authority. We are called to advocate for others, following the example of Jesus who advocated for the marginalized in his community: the demon possessed man,

the bleeding woman, the poor widow who gave all she had, and the woman with her alabaster jar of oil, among countless others.

Advocacy doesn't have to be a picket sign on a street corner. It's much more effective to advocate by being in relationship with our youth and modeling to others how to do the same. In the church, we become dual advocates, in part fighting for the safety and comfort of transgender individuals and in part championing the greatness of our God who fiercely loves the creation God made.

Being an advocate isn't always easy, and there are several ways to do it wrong. For example, one time I was invited to teach a sexuality course at a youth group outside of my context and experience. I taught all the things I would have taught at one of my urban churches, including an "honest answer" question box and video clips.

Then, without taking into consideration the context of this youth group, I showed a video that discussed different sexual and gender expressions. The blowback from this video that I thought was helpful and educational overshadowed most of the beneficial information and insights the youth might have gleaned. It ended up rocking the community and damaging the presence of the church in that town, as well as hurting my friend, the youth director who invited me in.

Out of that incredibly painful experience, I learned a few very important things; but first and foremost is the importance of knowing your context. Several of the suggestions I mentioned above are subtle; but if you have a student in your ministry who is out as transgender, people will be talking and asking questions. Knowing where your people are will help you guide conversations that will bring the church into a place that loves and supports that youth. If I could go back and do it again, I would have scaled back the amount of information I was presenting because it was too much all at once.

Gender-diverse people are still living in the shadows in many communities. Unfamiliarity with something can create fear of that thing. Fear can inhibit the ability to love—and to love with God's unconditional love, which is why education and relationships are so important.

From my own experiences, having one-on-one discussions with people who are upset about a transgender person participating in a church activity is the best way to proceed. Church meetings strip the individual of their humanity and make them an issue to be addressed instead of a person in need of community.

By already having an established culture in your youth ministry that promotes privacy, choice and agency, normalization, and affirmation of personhood, a youth and their family will feel more at ease walking into your church building, allowing greater opportunities for them to encounter God, just like Mary did. I pay close attention to my language, talking to both teens and adults; and it took a while for it to stick in my habits consistently. I also speak a lot about grace, forgiveness, and wholeness found in Jesus—messages that apply to all people, gender conforming or gender diverse.

By intentionally doing this, all people who walk into my ministry leave hearing a message that they are loved and that they belong. Developing a youth group culture that is welcoming begins with our example as leaders, modeling what it looks like to be the hands and feet of Jesus and inviting our volunteer youth leaders into the vision.

Step by Step
The church is an imperfect body attempting to bring the perfect kingdom of heaven here among the people God created. Every day, we do small things that teach us, challenge us, and stretch us to love God and love others more than we did the previous day. Being a youth worker doesn't require having all the answers. If it did, I sure wouldn't make the cut. But we pastor, we walk alongside our young people, and provide them a safety net that will catch them when they fall, hold them up when they are weak, and cheer them on as they triumph.

My letter from Mary hangs in my office behind my computer where I see it often. After I read her letter, she shared with me stories of her friend who is transgender and how they long for community but don't trust the church. Her heart breaks for them to have a place where they encounter the same God that she knows. I'm reminded that the small things I do in my ministry make a difference.

John Wesley lived by three simple rules: Do good, do no harm, and stay in love with God.[2] I've definitely caused harm, I haven't always done good, and I haven't always stayed in love with God, but I walk by faith and live in grace. Pastoring young people isn't for the faint of heart, and pastoring transgender youth is no different. We break down barriers to allow our students all equal access to a God who is chasing fervently after them.

---

2. From John Wesley's "Almost Christian," Sermon 2, preached at St. Mary's, Oxford, before the University on July 25, 1741.

GLOSSARY OF RELEVANT TERMS

Language is fluid, by nature, and always evolving. Paying attention to shifts in what is acceptable and what is derogatory may feel silly, too "politically correct," or simply frustrating to those unaffected by any of these descriptors and words. However, ministry to those identified here requires paying attention and making adjustments accordingly, so that our choice of words doesn't get in the way of our message. Having this vocabulary is also important to understanding the concerns and struggles of LGBTQ teens we encounter in our lives and ministries.

Note that many of these words (LGBTQ, queer, transgender, etc.) are appropriate as adjectives (*LGBTQ teenagers, a queer young person, a transgender woman*, etc.) but not always as nouns.

Binary: used to describe systems, language, and attitudes or beliefs that divide gender into only male and female

Bisexual/Bi: being emotionally and physically attracted to people who identify as male and/or female

Cis/Cisgender: describing a person whose gender identity aligns with the sex assigned to them at birth

Gay: being emotionally and sexually attracted to people of the same sex, but primarily used for male-to-male attraction

Gender Expression: the outward presentation of appearance or evidence of one's gender identity (can include: behavior, haircut, clothing, voice, social norms, etc.)

Gender Fluid: having a gender identity that is not fixed or binary

Gender Identity: a person's internal experience and perception of themselves as man, woman, a blend of both, or neither—may or may not align with the sex assigned to them at birth

Gender-Neutral: suitable for application to both male, female, and non-binary; describing words and expressions that can't be taken as only male or only female

Heterosexual: term for a person who is emotionally and physically attracted to people of the opposite sex; straight

Heteronormative: the assumption by society, institutions, or individuals that everyone is created heterosexual; may refer to the assumption upheld by many that only feminine women and masculine men are straight

Homosexual: term for a person emotionally and physically attracted to someone of the same sex; a term considered stigmatizing and often offensive today, particularly by many in the LGBTQ community because the term was controversially listed in the DSM (Diagnostic Manual of Mental Disorders) up until its removal in 1973, at which point it was determined by psychiatrists to *not* be a classification of mental illness

LGBTQ: abbreviation or acronym for the identifiers *lesbian, gay, bisexual, transgender*, and *queer* (or, alternately, *questioning*); as such, it is an identifier/adjective itself and not a noun

Lesbian: being emotionally and sexually attracted to a person of the same sex, but primarily used for female-to-female attraction

Queer: an umbrella term to describe individuals who don't identify as straight or heterosexual and/or have a non-normative gender identity; it's widely used in positive ways now in the LGBTQ community but because of its historical use as a derogatory term, some still find it controversial

Questioning: term used to describe one who is experiencing uncertainty regarding their sexual orientation *or* gender identity (appropriate to use as verb)

Same-Sex Attraction/SSA: having attraction to those of the same sex, with or without necessarily acting upon those feelings; sometimes "same-gender loving"

Sexual Orientation: the type of emotional and physical attraction one feels for others

Straight: see heterosexual

Transgender/Trans: describes a gender identity or expression that is different than the sex one was assigned at birth—does not imply sexual orientation (for example, transgender people may identify as straight, gay, lesbian, bi, etc.); preferred use is as an identifier/adjective, not as noun; an individual's preference of identifying as trans vs. transgender (or vice versa) should be noted and respected

MEET THE CONTRIBUTORS...

Shelley Donaldson is a youth worker, artist, writer, and LGBTQIA advocate, who holds a Master of Divinity from McCormick Theological Seminary. She has worked for advocacy groups and various PCUSA camps and churches in the US. In addition to spending much of her time doing hands-on ministry, speaking at conferences, leading workshops, and speaking about youth, Shelley can also be found traveling, writing, and working at Creation Lab (CreationLab.org). Her most recent work was published in *Growing in God's Love: A Story Bible* (Westminster John Knox). You can follow her adventures on her blog, TheTravellingTheologian.com.

Gemma Dunning is a Baptist minister with the Baptist Union of Great Britain and is based in London, England. With both undergraduate and postgrad studies that focus in applied theology and a JNC in youth work, Gemma is newly ordained, having undertaken her ministerial formation with Bristol Baptist College. Passionate about inclusion in the broadest sense, Gemma is a trustee of Cross Boarder Initiatives, a counter-trafficking initiative, and a pastoral facilitator with Diverse Church, an online support community for young adult LGBT+ Christians and their parents. Gemma is mum to two creative and inspiring teens and loves movies, cupcakes, and craftivism. For more, visit GemmaDunning.com.

Nick Elio serves as the family ministries pastor of Denver Community Church in Denver, Colorado. Working with students for over a decade in many contexts, Nick speaks from his experience in student ministry, from middle school to college, large and small. He studied sociology and psychology at the University of Colorado Denver and has been on the front lines of the changing tide with regard to the LGBTQ conversation and its impact on teenagers. Nick currently lives in Denver with his wife and their two boys. You can hear more from Nick and learn more about his student ministry insights at NickElio.com.

Audrua Welch Malvaez is the director of adult ministries at Plymouth Park United Methodist Church in Irving, Texas. With a decade of youth ministry experience, she is in process to become a certified youth worker in the United Methodist Church. Audrua is passionate about healthy, medically accurate sex education in churches; and in addition to leading workshops for local youth groups, she also trains other youth workers in the concept of sex-positive youth ministry. A native Houstonian, she's currently living in Dallas with her husband and two dogs, sings acapella in a women's barbershop chorus, and is an avid quilter.

Mark Oestreicher (Marko) is a veteran youth worker and founding partner in The Youth Cartel, which provides resources, training, and coaching for church youth workers. The author of dozens of books, including *Youth Ministry 3.0, Hopecasting,* and *Leading Without Power: 9 Paths to Non-Coercive Ministry Leadership,* Marko is a sought after speaker, writer, and consultant and served as president of Youth Specialties for eight years. Marko lives in San Diego with Jeannie, his wife of thirty-one years, and their two college-age kids, Riley and Max. You can read Marko's blog at WhyIsMarko.com.

Eric Woods is the pastor at Eagle Village, a residential treatment facility for abused, neglected, and delinquent youth. In his previous role as the retreats director at a large Christian camp, Eric partnered with over four hundred church youth ministries from diverse backgrounds. Eric has a degree in youth ministry from John Brown University and is (very) slowly plugging away at an MA in ministry leadership. He and his wife have three teenagers of their own and have fostered more than a dozen children. He also raises chickens in his backyard, does occasional consulting and speaking, and blogs about his experiences at EricDWoods.com.